THE HANDBOOK OF

SOAP MANUFACTURE

BY

W. H. SIMMONS, B.Sc. (LOND.), F.C.S.

AND

H. A. APPLETON

WITH TWENTY-SEVEN ILLUSTRATIONS

PREFACE

In the general advance of technical knowledge and research during the last decade, the Soap Industry has not remained stationary. While there has not perhaps been anything of a very revolutionary character, steady progress has still been made in practically all branches, and the aim of the present work is to describe the manufacture of Household and Toilet Soaps as carried out to-day in an up-to-date and well-equipped factory.

In the more scientific portions of the book, an acquaintance with the principles of elementary chemistry is assumed, and in this we feel justified, as in these days of strenuous competition, no soap-maker can hope to compete successfully with his rivals unless he has a sound theoretical as well as practical knowledge of the nature of the raw materials he uses, and the reactions taking place in the pan, or at other stages of the manufacture. We also venture to hope that the work may prove useful to Works' Chemists and other Analysts consulted in connection with this Industry.

At the same time, in the greater part of the book no chemical knowledge is necessary, the subject being treated in such a way that it is hoped those who are not directly engaged in the manufacture of soap, but who desire a general idea of the subject, will find it of value.

In the sections dealing with the composition and analysis of materials, temperatures are expressed in degrees Centigrade, these being now almost invariably used in scientific work. In the rest of the book, however, they are given in degrees Fahrenheit (the degrees Centigrade being also added in brackets), as in the majority of factories these are still used.

As regards strengths of solution, in some factories the use of Baumé degrees is preferred, whilst in others Twaddell degrees are the custom, and we have therefore given the two figures in all cases.

In the chapter dealing with Oils and Fats, their Saponification Equivalents are given in preference to Saponification Values, as it has been our practice for some years to express our results in this way, as suggested by Allen in *Commercial Organic Analysis*, and all our records, from which most of the figures for the chief oils and fats are taken, are so stated.

For the illustrations, the authors are indebted to Messrs. E. Forshaw & Son, Ltd., H. D. Morgan, and W. J. Fraser & Co., Ltd.

W. H. S.
H. A. A.

LONDON, *September*, 1908.

CONTENTS

CHAPTER I.

INTRODUCTION.

Definition of Soap—Properties—Hydrolysis—Detergent Action.

CHAPTER II.

CONSTITUTION OF OILS AND FATS, AND THEIR SAPONIFICATION

Researches of Chevreul and Berthelot—Mixed Glycerides—Modern Theories of Saponification—Hydrolysis accelerated by (1) HEAT OR ELECTRICITY, (2) FERMENTS, Castor-seed Ferment, Steapsin, Emulsin, and (3) CHEMICAL REAGENTS, Sulphuric Acid, Twitchell's Reagent, Hydrochloric Acid, Lime, Magnesia, Zinc Oxide, Soda and Potash.

CHAPTER III.

RAW MATERIALS USED IN SOAP-MAKING

Fats and Oils—Waste Fats—Fatty Acids—Less-known Oils and Fats of Limited Use—Various New Fats and Oils Suggested for Soap-making—Rosin—Alkali (Caustic and Carbonated)—Water—Salt—Soap-stock.

CHAPTER IV.

BLEACHING AND TREATMENT OF RAW MATERIALS INTENDED FOR SOAP-MAKING

Palm Oil—Cotton-seed Oil—Cotton-seed "Foots"—Vegetable Oils—Animal Fats—Bone Fat—Rosin.

CHAPTER V.

SOAP-MAKING

Classification of Soaps—Direct combination of Fatty Acids with Alkali—Cold Process Soaps—Saponification under Increased or Diminished Pressure—Soft Soap—Marine Soap—Hydrated Soaps, Smooth and Marbled—Pasting or Saponification—Graining Out—Boiling on Strength—Fitting—Curd Soaps—Curd Mottled—Blue and Grey Mottled Soaps—Milling Base—Yellow Household Soaps—Resting of Pans and Settling of Soap—Utilisation of Nigres—Transparent soaps—Saponifying Mineral Oil—Electrical Production of Soap.

CHAPTER VI.

TREATMENT OF SETTLED SOAP

Cleansing—Crutching—Liquoring of Soaps—Filling—Neutralising, Colouring and Perfuming—Disinfectant Soaps—Framing—Slabbing—Barring—Open and Close Piling—Drying—Stamping—Cooling.

CHAPTER VII.

TOILET, TEXTILE AND MISCELLANEOUS SOAPS

Toilet Soaps—Cold Process soaps—Settled Boiled Soaps—Remelted Soaps—Milled Soaps—Drying—Milling and Incorporating Colour, Perfume, or Medicament—Perfume—Colouring matter—Neutralising and

Superfatting Material—Compressing—Cutting—Stamping—Medicated Soaps—Ether Soap—Floating Soaps—Shaving Soaps—Textile Soaps—Soaps for Woollen, Cotton and Silk Industries—Patent Textile Soaps—Miscellaneous Soaps.

CHAPTER VIII.

SOAP PERFUMES

Essential Oils—Source and Preparation—Properties—Artificial and Synthetic Perfumes.

CHAPTER IX.

GLYCERINE MANUFACTURE AND PURIFICATION

Treatment of Lyes—Evaporation to Crude Glycerine—Distillation—Distilled and Dynamite Glycerine—Chemically Pure Glycerine—Animal Charcoal for Decolorisation—Glycerine obtained by other methods of Saponification—Yield of Glycerine from Fats and Oils.

CHAPTER X.

ANALYSIS OF RAW MATERIALS, SOAP, AND GLYCERINE

Fats and Oils—Alkalies and Alkali Salts—Essential Oils—Soap—Lyes—Crude Glycerine.

CHAPTER XI.

STATISTICS OF THE SOAP INDUSTRY

APPENDIX A.

COMPARISON OF DEGREES, TWADDELL AND BAUMÉ, WITH ACTUAL DENSITIES

APPENDIX B.

COMPARISON OF DIFFERENT THERMOMETRIC SCALES

APPENDIX C.

TABLE OF THE SPECIFIC GRAVITIES OF SOLUTIONS OF CAUSTIC SODA

APPENDIX D.

TABLE OF STRENGTH OF CAUSTIC POTASH SOLUTIONS AT 60° F.

CHAPTER I.

INTRODUCTION.

Definition of Soap—Properties—Hydrolysis—Detergent Action.

It has been said that the use of soap is a gauge of the civilisation of a nation, but though this may perhaps be in a great measure correct at the present day, the use of soap has not always been co-existent with civilisation, for according to Pliny (*Nat. Hist.*, xxviii., 12, 51) soap was first introduced into Rome from Germany, having been discovered by the Gauls, who used the product obtained by mixing goats' tallow and beech ash for giving a bright hue to the hair. In West Central Africa, moreover, the natives, especially the Fanti race, have been accustomed to wash themselves with soap prepared by mixing crude palm oil and water with the ashes of banana and plantain skins. The manufacture of soap seems to have flourished during the eighth century in Italy and Spain, and was introduced into France some five hundred years later, when factories were established at Marseilles for the manufacture of olive-oil soap. Soap does not appear to have been made in England until the fourteenth century, and the first record of soap manufacture in London is in 1524. From this time till the beginning of the nineteenth century the manufacture of soap developed very slowly, being essentially carried on by rule-of-thumb methods, but the classic researches of Chevreul on the constitution of fats at once placed the industry upon a scientific basis, and stimulated by Leblanc's discovery of a process for the commercial manufacture of caustic soda from common salt, the production of soap has advanced by leaps and bounds until it is now one of the most important of British industries.

Definition of Soap.—The word soap (Latin *sapo*, which is cognate with Latin *sebum*, tallow) appears to have been originally applied to the product obtained by treating tallow with ashes. In its strictly chemical sense it refers to combinations of fatty acids with metallic bases, a definition which includes not only sodium stearate, oleate and palmitate, which form the bulk of the soaps of commerce, but also the linoleates of lead, manganese, etc., used as driers, and various pharmaceutical preparations, *e.g.*, mercury oleate (*Hydrargyri oleatum*), zinc oleate and lead plaster, together with a number of other metallic salts of fatty acids. Technically speaking, however, the meaning of the term soap is considerably restricted, being generally limited to the combinations of fatty acids and alkalies, obtained by treating various animal or vegetable fatty matters, or the fatty acids derived therefrom, with soda or potash, the former giving hard soaps, the latter soft soaps.

The use of ammonia as an alkali for soap-making purposes has often been attempted, but owing to the ease with which the resultant soap is decomposed, it can scarcely be looked upon as a product of much commercial value.

H. Jackson has, however, recently patented (Eng. Pat. 6,712, 1906) the use of ammonium oleate for laundry work. This detergent is prepared in the wash-tub at the time of use, and it is claimed that goods are cleansed by merely immersing them in this solution for a short time and rinsing in fresh water.

Neither of the definitions given above includes the sodium and potassium salts of rosin, commonly called rosin soap, for the acid constituents of rosin have been shown to be aromatic, but in view of the analogous properties of these resinates to true soap, they are generally regarded as legitimate constituents of soap, having been used in Great

Britain since 1827, and receiving legislative sanction in Holland in 1875.

Other definitions of soap have been given, based not upon its composition, but upon its properties, among which may be mentioned that of Kingzett, who says that "Soap, considered commercially, is a body which on treatment with water liberates alkali," and that of Nuttall, who defines soap as "an alkaline or unctuous substance used in washing and cleansing".

Properties of Soap.—Both soda and potash soaps are readily soluble in either alcohol or hot water. In cold water they dissolve more slowly, and owing to slight decomposition, due to hydrolysis (*vide infra*), the solution becomes distinctly turbid. Sodium oleate is peculiar in not undergoing hydrolysis except in very dilute solution and at a low temperature. On cooling a hot soap solution, a jelly of more or less firm consistence results, a property possessed by colloidal bodies, such as starch and gelatine, in contradistinction to substances which under the same conditions deposit crystals, due to diminished solubility of the salt at a lower temperature.

Krafft (*Journ. Soc. Chem. Ind.*, 1896, 206, 601; 1899, 691; and 1902, 1301) and his collaborators, Wiglow, Strutz and Funcke, have investigated this property of soap solutions very fully, the researches extending over several years. In the light of their more recent work, the molecules, or definite aggregates of molecules, of solutions which become gelatinous on cooling move much more slowly than the molecules in the formation of a crystal, but there is a definite structure, although arranged differently to that of a crystal. In the case of soda soaps the colloidal character increases with the molecular weight of the fatty acids.

Soda soaps are insoluble in concentrated caustic lyes, and, for the most part, in strong solutions of sodium chloride, hence the addition of caustic soda or brine to a solution of soda soap causes the soap to separate out and rise to the surface. Addition of brine to a solution of potash soap, on the other hand, merely results in double decomposition, soda soap and potassium chloride being formed, thus:—

$$C_{17}H_{35}COOK + NaCl = C_{17}H_{35}COONa + KCl$$

potassium stearate	sodium chloride	sodium stearate	potassium chloride

The solubility of the different soaps in salt solution varies very considerably. Whilst sodium stearate is insoluble in a 5 per cent. solution of sodium chloride, sodium laurate requires a 17 per cent. solution to precipitate it, and sodium caproate is not thrown out of solution even by a saturated solution.

Hydrolysis of Soap.—The term "hydrolysis" is applied to any resolution of a body into its constituents where the decomposition is brought about by the action of water, hence when soap is treated with *cold* water, it is said to undergo hydrolysis, the reaction taking place being represented in its simplest form by the equation:—

$$2NaC_{18}H_{35}O_2 + H_2O = NaOH + HNa(C_{18}H_{35}O_2)_2$$

sodium stearate	water	caustic soda	acid sodium stearate

The actual reaction which occurs has been the subject of investigation by many chemists, and very diverse conclusions have been arrived at. Chevreul, the pioneer in the modern chemistry of oils and fats, found that a small amount of alkali was liberated, as appears in the above equation, together with the formation of an acid salt, a very minute quantity of free fatty acid remaining in solution. Rotondi (*Journ. Soc. Chem. Ind.*, 1885, 601), on the other hand, considered that a neutral soap, on being dissolved in water, was resolved into a basic and an acid salt, the former readily soluble in both hot and cold water, the latter insoluble in cold water, and only slightly soluble in hot water. He appears, however, to have been misled by the fact that sodium oleate is readily soluble in cold water, and his views have been shown to be incorrect by Krafft and Stern (*Ber. d. Chem. Ges.*, 1894, 1747 and 1755), who from experiments with pure sodium palmitate and stearate entirely confirm the conclusions arrived at by Chevreul.

The extent of dissociation occurring when a soap is dissolved in water depends upon the nature of the fatty acids from which the soap is made, and also on the concentration of the solution. The sodium salts of cocoa-nut fatty acids (capric, caproic and caprylic acids) are by far the most easily hydrolysed, those of oleic acid and the fatty acids from cotton-seed oil being dissociated more readily than those of stearic acid and tallow fatty acids. The decomposition increases with the amount of water employed.

The hydrolytic action of water on soap is affected very considerably by the presence of certain substances dissolved in the water, particularly salts of calcium and magnesium. Caustic soda exerts a marked retarding effect on the hydrolysis, as do also ethyl and amyl alcohols and glycerol.

Detergent Action of Soap.—The property possessed by soap of removing dirt is one which it is difficult to satisfactorily explain. Many theories, more or less complicated, have been suggested, but even now the question cannot be regarded as solved.

The explanation commonly accepted is that the alkali liberated by hydrolysis attacks any greasy matter on the surface to be cleansed, and, as the fat is dissolved, the particles of dirt are loosened and easily washed off. Berzelius held this view, and considered that the value of a soap depended upon the ease with which it yielded free alkali on solution in water.

This theory is considered by Hillyer (*Journ. Amer. Chem. Soc.*, 1903, 524), however, to be quite illogical, for, as he points out, the liberated alkali would be far more likely to recombine with the acid or acid salt from which it has been separated, than to saponify a neutral glyceride, while, further, unsaponifiable greasy matter is removed by soap as easily as saponifiable fat, and there can be no question of any chemical action of the free alkali in its case. Yet another argument against the theory is that hydrolysis is greater in cold and dilute solutions, whereas hot concentrated soap solutions are generally regarded as having the best detergent action.

Rotondi (*Journ. Soc. Chem. Ind.*, 1885, 601) was of the opinion that the basic soap, which he believed to be formed by hydrolysis, was alone responsible for the detergent action of soap, this basic soap dissolving fatty matter by saponification, but, as already pointed out, his theory of the formation of a basic soap is now known to be incorrect, and his conclusions are therefore invalid.

Several explanations have been suggested, based on the purely physical properties of soap solutions. Most of these are probably, at any rate in part, correct, and there can be little doubt that the ultimate solution of the problem lies in this direction, and that the detergent action of soap will be found to depend on many of these properties, together with other factors not yet known.

Jevons in 1878 in some researches on the "Brownian movement" or "pedesis" of small particles, a movement of the particles which is observed to take place when clay, iron oxide, or other finely divided insoluble matter is suspended in water, found that the pedetic action was considerably increased by soap and sodium silicate, and suggested that to this action of soap might be attributed much of its cleansing power.

Alder Wright considered that the alkali liberated by hydrolysis in some way promoted contact of the water with the substance to be cleansed, and Knapp regarded the property of soap solutions themselves to facilitate contact of the water with the dirt, as one of the chief causes of the efficacy of soap as a detergent.

Another way in which it has been suggested that soap acts as a cleanser is that the soap itself or the alkali set free by hydrolysis serves as a lubricant, making the dirt less adherent, and thus promoting its removal.

The most likely theory yet advanced is that based on the emulsifying power of soap solutions. The fact that these will readily form emulsions with oils has long been known, and the detergent action of soap has frequently been attributed to it, the explanation given being that the alkali set free by the water emulsifies the fatty matter always adhering to dirt, and carries it away in suspension with the other impurities. Experiments by Hillyer (*loc. cit.*) show, however, that while N/10 solution of alkali will readily emulsify a cotton-seed oil containing free acidity, no emulsion is produced with an oil from which all the acidity has been removed, or with kerosene, whereas a N/10 solution of sodium oleate will readily give an emulsion with either, thus proving that the emulsification is due to the soap itself, and not to the alkali.

Plateau (*Pogg. Ann.*, 141, 44) and Quincke (*Wiedmann's. Ann.*, 35, 592) have made very complete researches on the emulsification and foaming of liquids and on the formation of bubbles. The former considers that there are two properties of a liquid which play an important part in the phenomenon, (1) it must have considerable viscosity, and (2) its surface tension must be low. Quincke holds similar views, but considers that no pure liquid will foam.

Soap solution admirably fulfils Plateau's second condition, its surface tension being only about 40 per cent. of that of water, while its cohesion is also very small; and it is doubtless to this property that its emulsifying power is chiefly due. So far as viscosity is concerned, this can have but little influence, for a 1 per cent. solution of sodium oleate, which has a viscosity very little different from that of pure water, is an excellent emulsifying agent.

Hillyer, to whose work reference has already been made, investigated the whole question of detergent action very exhaustively, and, as the result of a very large number of experiments, concludes that the cleansing power of soap is largely or entirely to be explained by the power which it has of emulsifying oily substances, of wetting and penetrating into oily textures, and of lubricating texture and impurities so that these may be removed easily. It is thought that all these properties may be explained by taking into account the low cohesion of the soap solutions, and their strong attraction or affinity to oily matter, which together cause the low surface tension between soap solution and oil.

CHAPTER II.

CONSTITUTION OF OILS AND FATS, AND THEIR SAPONIFICATION.

Researches of Chevreul and Berthelot—Mixed Glycerides—Modern Theories of Saponification—Hydrolysis accelerated by (1) Heat or Electricity, (2) Ferments; Castor-seed Ferment, Steapsin, Emulsin, and (3) Chemical Reagents; Sulphuric Acid, Twitchell's Reagent, Hydrochloric Acid, Lime, Magnesia, Zinc Oxide, Soda and Potash.

The term oil is of very wide significance, being applied to substances of vastly different natures, both organic and inorganic, but so far as soap-making materials are concerned, it may be restricted almost entirely to the products derived from animal and vegetable sources, though many attempts have been made during the last few years to also utilise mineral oils for the preparation of soap. Fats readily become oils on heating beyond their melting points, and may be regarded as frozen oils.

Although Scheele in 1779 discovered that in the preparation of lead plaster glycerol is liberated, soap at that time was regarded as a mere mechanical mixture, and the constitution of oils and fats was not properly understood. It was Chevreul who showed that the manufacture of soap involved a definite chemical decomposition of the oil or fat into fatty acid and glycerol, the fatty acid combining with soda, potash, or other base, to form the soap, and the glycerol remaining free. The reactions with stearin and palmitin (of which tallow chiefly consists) and with olein (found largely in olive and cotton-seed oils) are as follows:—

$$\begin{array}{l} CH_2OOC_{18}H_{35} \\ | \\ CHOOC_{18}H_{35} + 3NaOH = 3NaOOC_{18}H_{35} + \\ | \\ CH_2OOC_{18}H_{35} \end{array} \quad \begin{array}{l} CH_2OH \\ | \\ CHOH \\ | \\ CH_2OH \end{array}$$

stearin — sodium hydroxide — sodium stearate — glycerol

$$\begin{array}{l} CH_2OOC_{16}H_{31} \\ | \\ CHOOC_{16}H_{31} + 3NaOH = 3NaOOC_{16}H_{31} + \\ | \\ CH_2OOC_{16}H_{31} \end{array} \quad \begin{array}{l} CH_2OH \\ | \\ CHOH \\ | \\ CH_2OH \end{array}$$

palmitin — sodium hydroxide — sodium palmitate — glycerol

$$\begin{array}{l} CH_2OOC_{18}H_{33} \\ | \\ CHOOC_{18}H_{33} + 3NaOH = 3NaOOC_{18}H_{33} + \\ | \\ CH_2OOC_{18}H_{33} \end{array} \quad \begin{array}{l} CH_2OH \\ | \\ CHOH \\ | \\ CH_2OH \end{array}$$

olein — sodium hydroxide — sodium oleate — glycerol

Berthelot subsequently confirmed Chevreul's investigations by directly synthesising the fats from fatty acids and glycerol, the method he adopted consisting in heating the fatty acids with glycerol in sealed tubes. Thus, for example:—

$$3C_{18}H_{35}O_2H + C_3H_5(OH)_3 = C_3H_5(C_{18}H_{35}O_2)_3$$
stearic acid   glycerol   tristearin

Since glycerol is a trihydric alcohol, *i.e.*, contains three hydroxyl (OH) groups, the hydrogen atoms of which are displaceable by acid radicles, the above reaction may be supposed to take place in three stages. Thus, we may have:—

(1) $C_{18}H_{35}O_2H + C_3H_5(OH)_3 = C_3H_5(OH)_2C_{18}H_{35}O_2 + H_2O$
monostearin

(2) $C_{18}H_{35}O_2H + C_3H_5(OH)_2C_{18}H_{35}O_2 = C_3H_5(OH)(C_{18}H_{35}O_2)_2 + H_2O$
distearin

(3) $C_{18}H_{35}O_2H + C_3H_5(OH)(C_{18}H_{35}O_2)_2 = C_3H_5(C_{18}H_{35}O_2)_3 + H_2O$
tristearin

There are two possible forms of monoglyceride and diglyceride, according to the relative position of the acid radicle, these being termed alpha and beta respectively, and represented by the following formulæ, where R denotes the acid radicle:—

Monoglyceride:—

$$\begin{array}{cc} CH_2OR & CH_2OH \\ | & | \\ (alpha)\ CHOH\ \ and\ (beta)\ CHOR \\ | & | \\ CH_2OH & CH_2OH \end{array}$$

Diglyceride:—

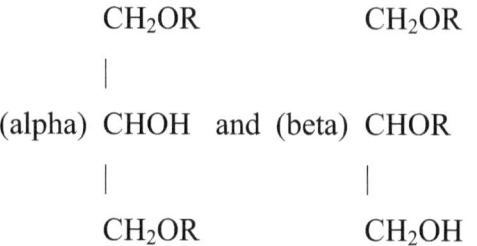

According to the relative proportions of fatty acid and glycerol used, and the temperature to which they were heated, Berthelot succeeded in preparing mono-, di- and triglycerides of various fatty acids.

Practically all the oils and fats used in soap-making consist of mixtures of these compounds of glycerol with fatty acids, which invariably occur in nature in the form of triglycerides.

It was formerly considered that the three acid radicles in any naturally occurring glyceride were identical, corresponding to the formula—

where R denotes the acid radicle. Recent work, however, has shown the existence of several so-called *mixed glycerides*, in which the hydroxyls of the same molecule of glycerol are displaced by two or sometimes three different acid radicles.

The first mixed glyceride to be discovered was oleodistearin, $C_3H_5(OC_{18}H_{35}O)(OC_{18}H_{35}O)_2$, obtained by

Heise in 1896 from Mkani fat. Hansen has since found that tallow contains

oleodipalmitin, $C_3H_5(OC_{18}H_{35}O)(OC_{16}H_{31}O)$,
stearodipalmitin, $C_3H_5(OC_{18}H_{35}O)(OC_{16}H_{31}O)$,
oleopalmitostearin, $C_3H_5(OC_{18}H_{33}O)(OC_{16}H_{31}O)$
$(OC_{18}H_{35}O)$ and

palmitodistearin, $CH(OC_{16}H_{31}O)(OC_{18}H_{35}O)_2$,

the latter of which has also been obtained by Kreis and Hafner from lard, while Holde and Stange have shown that olive oil contains from 1 to 2 per cent. of oleodidaturin, $C_3H_5(OC_{18}H_{33}O)(OC_{17}H_{33}O)_2$, and Hehner and Mitchell have obtained indications of mixed glycerides in linseed oil (which they consider contains a compound of glycerol with two radicles of linolenic acid and one radicle of oleic acid), also in cod-liver, cod, whale and shark oils.

In some cases the fatty acids are combined with other bases than glycerol. As examples may be cited beeswax, containing myricin or myricyl palmitate, and spermaceti, consisting chiefly of cetin or cetyl palmitate, and herein lies the essential difference between fats and waxes, but as these substances are not soap-making materials, though sometimes admixed with soap to accomplish some special object, they do not require further consideration.

The principal pure triglycerides, with their formulæ and chief constants, are given in the following table:—

Glyceride.	Formula.	Chief Occurrence.	Melting Point, °C.	Refractive Index at 60° C.	Saponification Equivalent.
Butyrin	$C_3H_5(O.C_4H_7O)_3$	Butter fat	Liquid at -60	1.42015	100.7
Isovalerin	$C_3H_5(O.C_5H_9O)_3$	Porpoise, dolphin	...	...	114.7
Caproin	$C_3H_5(O.C_6H_{11}O)_3$	Cocoa-nut and palm-nut oils	-25	1.42715	128.7
Caprylin	$C_3H_5(O.C_8H_{15}O)_3$	Do. do.	-8.3	1.43316	156.7
Caprin	$C_3H_5(O.C_{10}H_{19}O)_3$	Do. do.	31.1	1.43697	184.7
Laurin	$C_3H_5(O.C_{12}H_{23}O)_3$	Do. do.	45	1.44039	212.7
Myristin	$C_3H_5(O.C_{14}H_{27}O)_3$	Nutmeg butter	56.5	1.44285	240.7
Palmitin	$C_3H_5(O.C_{16}H_{31}O)_3$	Palm oil, lard	63-64	...	268.7
Stearin	$C_3H_5(O.C_{18}H_{35}O)_3$	Tallow, lard, cacao butter	71.6	...	296.7
Olein	$C_3H_5(O.C_{18}H_{33}O)_3$	Olive and almond oils	Solidifies at -6	...	294.7
Ricinolein	$C_3H_5(O.C_{18}H_{33}O_2)_3$	Castor oil	...	...	310.7

Of the above the most important from a soap-maker's point of view are stearin, palmitin, olein and laurin, as these predominate in the fats and oils generally used in that industry. The presence of stearin and palmitin, which are solid at the ordinary temperature, gives firmness to a fat; the greater the percentage present, the harder the fat and the higher will be the melting point, hence tallows and palm oils are solid, firm fats. Where olein, which is liquid, is the chief constituent, we have softer fats, such as lard, and liquid oils, as almond, olive and cotton-seed.

Stearin (Tristearin) can be prepared from tallow by crystallisation from a solution in ether, forming small crystals which have a bright pearly lustre. The melting point of stearin appears to undergo changes and suggests the existence of distinct modifications. When heated to 55° C. stearin liquefies; with increase of temperature it becomes solid, and again becomes liquid at 71.6° C. If this liquid be further heated to 76° C., and allowed to cool, it will not solidify until 55° C. is reached, but if the liquid at 71.6° C. be allowed to cool, solidification will occur at 70° C.

Palmitin (Tripalmitin) may be obtained by heating together palmitic acid and glycerol, repeatedly boiling the resulting product with strong alcohol, and allowing it to crystallise. Palmitin exists in scales, which have a peculiar pearly appearance, and are greasy to the touch. After melting and solidifying, palmitin shows no crystalline fracture; when heated to 46° C. it melts to a liquid which becomes solid on further heating, again liquefying when 61.7° C. is reached, and becoming cloudy, with separation of crystalline particles. At 63° C. it is quite clear, and this temperature is taken as the true melting point. It has been suggested that the different changes at the temperatures mentioned are due to varying manipulation, such as rate at which the temperature is raised, and the initial temperature of the mass when previously cool.

Olein (Triolein) is an odourless, colourless, tasteless oil, which rapidly absorbs oxygen and becomes rancid. It has been prepared synthetically by heating glycerol and oleic acid together, and may be obtained by submitting olive oil to a low temperature for several days, when the liquid portion may be further deprived of any traces of stearin and palmitin by dissolving in alcohol. Olein may be distilled *in vacuo* without decomposition taking place.

Laurin (Trilaurin) may be prepared synthetically from glycerol and lauric acid. It crystallises in needles, melting at 45°-46° C., which are readily soluble in ether, but only slightly so in cold absolute alcohol. Scheij gives its specific gravity, $d 60°/4° = 0.8944$. Laurin is the chief constituent of palm-kernel oil, and also one of the principal components of cocoa-nut oil.

Fatty Acids.—When a fat or oil is saponified with soda or potash, the resulting soap dissolved in hot water, and sufficient dilute sulphuric acid added to decompose the soap, an oily layer gradually rises to the surface of the liquid, which, after clarifying by warming and washing free from mineral acid, is soluble in alcohol and reddens blue litmus paper. This oily layer consists of the "fatty acids" or rather those insoluble in water, acids like acetic, propionic, butyric, caproic, caprylic and capric, which are all more or less readily soluble in water, remaining for the most part dissolved in the aqueous portion. All the acids naturally present in oils and fats, whether free or combined, are monobasic in character, that is to say, contain only one carboxyl—CO.OH group. The more important fatty acids may be classified according to their chemical constitution into five homologous series, having the general formulæ:—

I. Stearic series $C_nH_{2n+1}COOH$
II. Oleic series $C_nH_{2n-1}COOH$
III. Linolic series $C_nH_{2n-3}COOH$
IV. Linolenic series $C_nH_{2n-5}COOH$
V. Ricinoleic series $C_nH_{2n-7}COOH$

I. *Stearic Series.*—The principal acids of this series, together with their melting points and chief sources, are given in the following table:—

Acid.	Formula.	Melting Point, °C.	Found in
Acetic	CH_3COOH	17	Macassar oil.
Butyric	C_3H_7COOH	...	Butter, Macassar oil.
Isovaleric	C_4H_9COOH	...	Porpoise and dolphin oils.
Caproic	$C_5H_{11}COOH$	...	Butter, cocoa-nut oil.
Caprylic	$C_7H_{15}COOH$	15	Butter, cocoa-nut oil, Limburg cheese.
Capric	$C_9H_{19}COOH$	30	Butter, cocoa-nut oil.
Lauric	$C_{11}H_{23}COOH$	44	Cocoa-nut oil, palm-kernel oil.
Ficocerylic	$C_{12}H_{25}COOH$	...	Pisang wax.
Myristic	$C_{13}H_{27}COOH$	54	Nutmeg butter, liver fat, cocoa-nut oil, dika fat, croton oil.
Palmitic	$C_{15}H_{31}COOH$	62.5	Palm oil, most animal fats.
Daturic	$C_{16}H_{33}COOH$	...	Oil of Datura Stramonium.
Stearic	$C_{17}H_{35}COOH$	69	Tallow, lard,

			most solid animal fats.
Arachidic	$C_{19}H_{39}COOH$	75	Arachis or earth-nut oil, rape and mustard-seed oils.
Behenic	$C_{21}H_{43}COOH$	...	Ben oil, black mustard-seed oil, rape oil.
Lignoceric	$C_{23}H_{47}COOH$	80.5	Arachis oil.
Carnaubic	$C_{23}H_{47}COOH$	...	Carnauba wax.
Pisangcerylic	$C_{23}H_{47}COOH$	...	Pisang wax.
Hyænic	$C_{24}H_{49}COOH$	...	Hyæna fat.
Cerotic	$C_{25}H_{51}COOH$	78	Beeswax, China wax, spermaceti.
Melissic	$C_{29}H_{59}COOH$	89	Beeswax.
Psyllostearylic	$C_{32}H_{65}COOH$	...	Psylla wax.
Theobromic	$C_{63}H_{127}COOH$	...	Cacao butter

Medullic and margaric acids, which were formerly included in this series, have now been shown to consist of mixtures of stearic and palmitic, and stearic palmitic and oleic acids respectively.

The acids of this group are saturated compounds, and will not combine directly with iodine or bromine. The two first are liquid at ordinary temperatures, distil without decomposition, and are miscible with water in all proportions; the next four are more or less soluble in water and distil unchanged in the presence of water, as does also lauric acid, which is almost insoluble in cold water, and only slightly dissolved by boiling water. The higher acids of the series are solid, and are completely insoluble in water. All these acids are soluble in warm alcohol, and on being heated with solid caustic alkali undergo no change.

II. *Oleic Series:*—

Acid.	Formula.	Melting Point, °C.	Found in
Tiglic	C_4H_7COOH	64.5	Croton oil.
Moringic	$C_{14}H_{27}COOH$	0	Ben oil.
Physetoleic	$C_{15}H_{29}COOH$	30	Sperm oil.
Hypogæic	$C_{15}H_{29}COOH$	33	Arachis and maize oils.
Oleic	$C_{17}H_{33}COOH$	14	Most oils and fats.
Rapic	$C_{17}H_{33}COOH$	...	Rape oil.
Doeglic	$C_{18}H_{35}COOH$	...	Bottle-nose oil.
Erucic	$C_{21}H_{41}COOH$	34	Mustard oils, marine animal oils, rape oil.

The unsaturated nature of these acids renders their behaviour with various reagents entirely different from that of the preceding series. Thus, they readily combine with bromine or iodine to form addition compounds, and the lower members of the series are at once reduced, on treatment with sodium amalgam in alkaline solution, to the corresponding saturated acids of Series I. Unfortunately, this reaction does not apply to the higher acids such as oleic acid, but as the conversion of the latter into solid acids is a matter of some technical importance from the point of view of the candle-maker, a number of attempts have been made to effect this by other methods.

De Wilde and Reychler have shown that by heating oleic acid with 1 per cent. of iodine in autoclaves up to 270°-280° C., about 70 per cent. is converted into stearic acid, and Zürer has devised (German Patent 62,407) a process whereby the oleic acid is first converted by the action of chlorine into the dichloride, which is then reduced with nascent hydrogen. More recently Norman has secured a patent (English Patent 1,515, 1903) for the conversion of unsaturated fatty acids of Series II. into the saturated compounds of Series I., by reduction with hydrogen or water-gas in the presence of finely divided nickel, cobalt or iron. It is claimed that by this method oleic acid is completely transformed into stearic acid, and that the melting point of tallow fatty acids is raised thereby about 12° C.

Another method which has been proposed is to run the liquid olein over a series of electrically charged plates, which effects its reduction to stearin.

Stearic acid is also formed by treating oleic acid with fuming hydriodic acid in the presence of phosphorus, while other solid acids are obtained by the action of sulphuric acid or zinc chloride on oleic acid.

Acids of Series II. may also be converted into saturated acids by heating to 300°C. with solid caustic potash, which decomposes them into acids of the stearic series with liberation of hydrogen. This reaction, with oleic acid, for example, is generally represented by the equation—

$$C_{18}H_{34}O_2 + 2KOH = KC_2H_3O_2 + KC_{16}H_{31}O_2 + H_2,$$

though it must be really more complex than this indicates, for, as Edmed has pointed out, oxalic acid is also formed in considerable quantity. The process on a commercial scale has now been abandoned.

One of the most important properties of this group of acids is the formation of isomeric acids of higher melting point on treatment with nitrous acid, generally termed the *elaidin reaction*. Oleic acid, for example, acted upon by nitrous acid, yields elaidic acid, melting at 45°, and erucic acid gives brassic acid, melting at 60°C. This reaction also occurs with the neutral glycerides of these acids, olein being converted into elaidin, which melts at 32°C.

The lead salts of the acids of this series are much more soluble in ether, and the lithium salts more soluble in alcohol than those of the stearic series, upon both of which properties processes have been based for the separation of the solid from the liquid fatty acids.

III. *Linolic Series:*—

Acid.	Formula.	Melting Point, °C.	Found in
Elæomargaric	$C_{16}H_{29}COOH$	...	Chinese-wood oil.
Elæostearic	$C_{16}H_{29}COOH$	71	Chinese-wood oil.
Linolic	$C_{17}H_{31}COOH$	Fluid	Linseed, cotton-seed and maize oils.
Tariric	$C_{17}H_{31}COOH$	50.5	Tariri-seed oil.
Telfairic	$C_{17}H_{31}COOH$	Fluid	Telfairia oil.

These acids readily combine with bromine, iodine, or oxygen. They are unaffected by nitrous acid, and their lead salts are soluble in ether.

IV. *Linolenic Series:*—

Acid.	Formula.	Found in
Linolenic	$C_{17}H_{29}COOH$	Linseed oil.
Isolinolenic	$C_{17}H_{29}COOH$	Linseed oil.
Jecoric	$C_{17}H_{29}COOH$	Cod-liver and marine animal oils.

These acids are similar in properties to those of Class III., but combine with six atoms of bromine or iodine, whereas the latter combine with only four atoms.

V. *Ricinoleic Series:*—

Acid.	Formula.	Melting Point, °C.	Found in
Ricinoleic	$C_{17}H_{22}(OH)COOH$	4-5	Castor oil.

This acid combines with two atoms of bromine or iodine, and is converted by nitrous acid into the isomeric ricinelaidic acid, which melts at 52°-53° C. Pure ricinoleic acid, obtained from castor oil, is optically active, its rotation being α_d +6° 25'.

Hydrolysis or Saponification of Oils and Fats.—The decomposition of a triglyceride, brought about by caustic alkalies in the formation of soap, though generally represented by the equation already given (pp. 6 and 7)—

$C_3H_5(OR) + 3NaOH = C_3H_5(OH)_3 + 3RONa,$

is not by any means such a simple reaction.

In the first place, though in this equation no water appears, the presence of the latter is found to be indispensable for saponification to take place; in fact, the water must be regarded as actually decomposing the oil or fat, caustic soda or potash merely acting as a catalytic agent. Further, since in the glycerides there are three acid radicals to be separated from glycerol, their saponification can be supposed to take place in three successive stages, which are the converse of the formation of mono- and diglycerides in the synthesis of triglycerides from fatty acids and glycerine. Thus, the above equation may be regarded as a summary of the following three:—

(i.) $C_3H_5 \begin{cases} OR \\ OR \\ OR \end{cases} + NaOH = C_3H_5 \begin{cases} OH \\ OR \\ OR \end{cases} + RONa$

(ii.) $C_3H_5 \begin{cases} OH \\ OR \\ OR \end{cases} + NaOH = C_3H_5 \begin{cases} OH \\ OR \\ OH \end{cases} + RONa$

(iii.) $C_3H_5 \begin{cases} OH \\ OR \\ OH \end{cases} + NaOH = C_3H_5 \begin{cases} OH \\ OH \\ OH \end{cases} + RONa$

Geitel and Lewkowitsch, who have studied this question from the physical and chemical point of view respectively, are of opinion that when an oil or fat is saponified, these three reactions do actually occur side by side, the soap-pan containing at the same time unsaponified triglyceride, diglyceride, monoglyceride, glycerol and soap.

This theory is not accepted, however, by all investigators. Balbiano and Marcusson doubt the validity of Lewkowitsch's conclusions, and Fanto, experimenting on the saponification of olive oil with caustic potash, is unable to detect the intermediate formation of any mono- or diglyceride, and concludes that in homogeneous solution the saponification is practically quadrimolecular. Kreeman, on the other hand, from physico-chemical data, supports the view of Geitel and Lewkowitsch that saponification is bimolecular, and though the evidence seems to favour this theory, the matter cannot be regarded as yet definitely settled.

Hydrolysis can be brought about by water alone, if sufficient time is allowed, but as the process is extremely slow, it is customary in practice to accelerate the reaction by the use of various methods, which include (i.) the application of heat or electricity, (ii.) action of enzymes, and (iii.) treatment with chemicals; the accelerating effect of the two latter methods is due to their emulsifying power.

The most usual method adopted in the manufacture of soap is to hydrolyse the fat or oil by caustic soda or potash, the fatty acids liberated at the same time combining with the catalyst, *i.e.*, soda or potash, to form soap. Hitherto the other processes of hydrolysis have been employed chiefly for the preparation of material for candles, for which purpose complete separation of the glycerol in the first hydrolysis is not essential, since the fatty matter is usually subjected to a second treatment with sulphuric acid to increase the proportion of solid fatty acids. The colour of the resulting fatty acids is also of no importance, as they are always subjected to distillation.

During the last few years, however, there has been a growing attempt to first separate the glycerol from the fatty acids, and then convert the latter into soap by treatment with the carbonates of soda or potash, which are of course considerably cheaper than the caustic alkalies, but cannot be used in the actual saponification of a neutral fat. The two processes chiefly used for this purpose are those in which the reaction is brought about by enzymes or by Twitchell's reagent.

I. *Application of Heat or Electricity.*—Up to temperatures of 150° C. the effect of water on oils and fats is very slight, but by passing superheated steam through fatty matter heated to 200°-300° C. the neutral glycerides are completely decomposed into glycerol and fatty acids according to the equation—

$$C_3H_5(OR)_3 + 3H.OH = C_3H_5(OH)_3 + 3ROH.$$

The fatty acids and glycerol formed distil over with the excess of steam, and by arranging a series of condensers, the former, which condense first, are obtained almost alone in the earlier ones, and an aqueous solution of glycerine in the later ones. This method of preparation of fatty acids is extensively used in France for the production of stearine for candle-manufacture, but the resulting product is liable to be dark coloured, and to yield a dark soap. To expose the acids to heat for a minimum of time, and so prevent discoloration, Mannig has patented (Germ. Pat. 160,111) a process whereby steam under a pressure of 8 to 10 atmospheres is projected against a baffle plate mounted in a closed vessel, where it mixes with the fat or oil in the form of a spray, the rate of hydrolysis being thereby, it is claimed, much increased.

Simpson (Fr. Pat. 364,587) has attempted to accelerate further the decomposition by subjecting oils or fats to the simultaneous action of heat and electricity. Superheated steam is passed into the oil, in which are immersed the two electrodes connected with a dynamo or battery, the temperature not being allowed to exceed 270° C.

II. *Action of Enzymes.*—It was discovered by Muntz in 1871 (*Annales de Chemie*, xxii.) that during germination of castor seeds a quantity of fatty acid was developed in the seeds, which he suggested might be due to the decomposition of the oil by the embryo acting as a ferment. Schutzenberger in 1876 showed that when castor seeds are steeped in water, fatty acids and glycerol are liberated, and attributed this to the hydrolytic action of an enzyme present in the seeds. No evidence of the existence of such a ferment was adduced, however, till 1890, when Green (*Roy. Soc. Proc.*, 48, 370) definitely proved the presence in the seeds of a ferment capable of splitting up the oil into fatty acid and glycerol.

The first experimenters to suggest any industrial application of this enzymic hydrolysis were Connstein, Hoyer and Wartenburg, who (*Berichte*, 1902, 35, pp. 3988-4006) published the results of a lengthy investigation of the whole subject. They found that tallow, cotton-seed, palm, olive, almond, and many other oils, were readily hydrolysed by the castor-seed ferment in the presence of dilute acid, but that cocoa-nut and palm-kernel oils only decomposed with difficulty. The presence of acidity is essential for the hydrolysis to take place, the most suitable strength being one-tenth normal, and the degree of hydrolysis is proportional to the quantity of ferment present. Sulphuric, phosphoric, acetic or butyric acids, or sodium bisulphate, may be used without much influence on the result. Butyric acid is stated to be the best, but in practice is too expensive, and acetic acid is usually adopted. The emulsified mixture should be allowed to stand for twenty-four hours, and the temperature should not exceed 40° C.; at 50° C. the action is weakened, and at 100° C. ceases altogether.

Several investigators have since examined the hydrolysing power of various other seeds, notably Braun and Behrendt (*Berichte*, 1903, 36, 1142-1145, 1900-1901, and 3003-3005), who, in addition to confirming Connstein, Hoyer and Wartenburg's work with castor seeds, have made similar experiments with jequirity seeds (*Abrus peccatorius*) containing the enzyme abrin, emulsin from crushed almonds, the leaves of *Arctostaphylos Uva Ursi*, containing the glucoside arbutin, myrosin from black mustard-seed, gold lac (*Cheirantus cheiri*) and crotin from croton seeds. Jequirity seeds were found to have a stronger decomposing action on lanoline and carnauba wax than the castor seed, but only caused decomposition of castor oil after the initial acidity was first neutralised with alkali. Neither emulsin, arbutin nor crotin have any marked hydrolytic action on castor oil, but myrosin is about half as active as castor seeds, except in the presence of potassium myronate, when no decomposition occurs.

S. Fokin (*J. russ. phys. chem. Ges.*, 35, 831-835, and *Chem. Rev. Fett. u. Harz. Ind.*, 1904, 30 *et seq.*) has examined the hydrolytic action of a large number of Russian seeds, belonging to some thirty different families, but although more than half of these brought about the hydrolysis of over 10 per cent. of fat, he considers that in only two cases, *viz.*, the seeds of *Chelidonium majus* and *Linaria vulgaris*, is the action due to enzymes, these being the only two seeds for which the yield of fatty acids is proportional to the amount of seed employed, while in many instances hydrolysis was not produced when the seeds were old. The seeds of *Chelidonium majus* were found to have as great, and possibly greater, enzymic activity than castor seeds, but those of *Linaria* are much weaker, twenty to thirty parts having only the same lipolytic activity as four to five parts of castor seeds.

The high percentage of free acids found in rice oil has led C. A. Brown, jun. (*Journ. Amer. Chem. Soc.*, 1903, 25, 948-954), to examine the rice bran, which proves to have considerable enzymic activity, and rapidly effects the hydrolysis of glycerides.

The process for the utilisation of enzymic hydrolysis in the separation of fatty acids from glycerine on the industrial scale, as originally devised by Connstein and his collaborators, consisted in rubbing a quantity of the coarsely crushed castor seeds with part of the oil or fat, then adding the rest of the oil, together with acidified water (N/10 acetic acid). The quantities employed were 6-1/2 parts of decorticated castor beans for every 100 parts of oil or fat, and 50 to 60 parts of acetic acid. After stirring until an emulsion is formed, the mixture is allowed to stand for twenty-four hours, during which hydrolysis takes place. The temperature is then raised to 70°-80° C., which destroys the enzyme, and a 25 per cent. solution of sulphuric acid, equal in amount to one-fiftieth of the total quantity of fat originally taken, added to promote separation of the fatty acids. In this way three layers are formed, the one at the top consisting of the clear fatty acids, the middle one an emulsion containing portions of the seeds, fatty acids and glycerine, and the bottom one consisting of the aqueous glycerine. The intermediate layer is difficult to treat satisfactorily; it is generally washed twice with water, the washings being added to glycerine water, and the fatty mixture saponified and the resultant soap utilised.

The process has been the subject of a considerable amount of investigation, numerous attempts having been made to actually separate the active fat-splitting constituent of the seeds, or to obtain it in a purer and more concentrated form than is furnished by the seeds themselves. Nicloux (*Comptes Rendus*, 1904, 1112, and *Roy. Soc. Proc.*, 1906, 77 B, 454) has shown that the hydrolytic activity of castor seeds is due entirely to the cytoplasm, which it is possible to separate by mechanical means from the aleurone grains and all other cellular matter. This active substance, which he terms "lipaseidine," is considered to be not an enzyme, though it acts as such, following the ordinary laws of enzyme action; its activity is destroyed by contact with water in the absence of oil. This observer has patented (Eng. Pat. 8,304, 1904) the preparation of an "extract" by triturating crushed castor or other seeds with castor oil, filtering the oily extract, and subjecting it to centrifugal force. The deposit consists of aleurone and the active enzymic substance, together with about 80 per cent. of oil, and one part of it will effect nearly complete hydrolysis of 100 parts of oil in twenty-four hours. In a subsequent addition to this patent, the active agent is separated from the aleurone by extraction with benzene and centrifugal force. By the use of such an extract, the quantity of albuminoids brought into contact with the fat is reduced to about 10 per cent. of that in the original seeds, and the middle layer between the glycerine solution and fatty acids is smaller and can be saponified directly for the production of curd soap, while the glycerine solution also is purer.

In a further patent Nicloux (Fr. Pat. 349,213, 1904) states that the use of an acid medium is unnecessary, and claims that even better results are obtained by employing a neutral solution of calcium sulphate containing a small amount of magnesium sulphate, the proportion of salts not exceeding 0.5 per cent. of the fat, while in yet another patent, jointly with Urbain (Fr. Pat. 349,942, 1904), it is claimed that the process is accelerated by the removal of acids from the oil or fat to be treated, which may be accomplished by either washing first with acidulated water, then with pure water, or preferably by neutralising with carbonate of soda and removing the resulting soap.

Lombard (Fr. Pat. 350,179, 1904) claims that acids act as stimulating agents in the enzymic hydrolysis of oils, and further that a simple method of obtaining the active product is to triturate oil cake with its own weight of water, allow the mixture to undergo spontaneous proteolytic hydrolysis at 40° C. for eight days, and then filter, the filtrate obtained being used in place of water in the enzymic process.

Hoyer, who has made a large number of experiments in the attempt to isolate the lipolytic substance from castor seeds, has obtained a product of great activity, which he terms "ferment-oil," by extracting the crushed seeds with a solvent for oils.

The Verein Chem. Werke have extended their original patent (addition dated 11th December, 1905, to Fr. Pat. 328,101, Oct., 1902), which now covers the use of vegetable ferments in the presence of water and manganese sulphate or other metallic salt. It is further stated that acetic acid may be added at the beginning of the operation, or use may be made of that formed during the process, though in the latter case hydrolysis is somewhat slower.

Experiments have been carried out by Lewkowitsch and Macleod (*Journ. Soc. Chem. Ind.*, 1903, 68, and *Proc. Roy. Soc.*, 1903, 31) with ferments derived from animal sources, *viz.*, lipase from pig's liver, and steapsin from the pig or ox pancreas. The former, although it has been shown by Kastle and Loevenhart (*Amer. Chem. Journ.*, 1900, 49) to readily hydrolyse ethyl butyrate, is found to have very little fat-splitting power, but with steapsin more favourable results have been obtained, though the yield of fatty acids in this case is considerably inferior to that given by castor seeds. With cotton-seed oil, 83-86 per cent. of fatty acids were liberated as a maximum after fifty-six days, but with lard only 46 per cent. were produced in the same time. Addition of dilute acid or alkali appeared to exert no influence on the decomposition of the cotton-seed oil, but in the case of the lard, dilute alkali seemed at first to promote hydrolysis, though afterwards to retard it.

Fokin (*Chem. Rev. Fett. u. Harz. Ind.*, 1904, 118-120 *et seq.*) has attempted to utilise the pancreatic juice on a technical scale, but the process proved too slow and too costly to have any practical use.

Rancidity.—The hydrolysing power of enzymes throws a good deal of light on the development of rancidity in oils and fats, which is now generally regarded as due to the oxidation by air in the presence of light and moisture of the free fatty acids contained by the oil or fat. It has long been known that whilst recently rendered animal fats are comparatively free from acidity, freshly prepared vegetable oils invariably contain small quantities of free fatty acid, and there can be no doubt that this must be attributed to the action of enzymes contained in the seeds or fruit from which the oils are expressed, hence the necessity for separating oils and fats from adhering albuminous matters as quickly as possible.

Decomposition of Fats by Bacteria.—Though this subject is not of any practical interest in the preparation of fatty acids for soap-making, it may be mentioned, in passing, that some bacteria readily hydrolyse fats. Schriber (*Arch. f. Hyg.*, 41, 328-347) has shown that in the presence of air many bacteria promote hydrolysis, under favourable conditions as to temperature and access of oxygen, the process going beyond the simple splitting up into fatty acid and glycerol, carbon dioxide and water being formed. Under anærobic conditions, however, only a slight primary hydrolysis was found to take place, though according to Rideal (*Journ. Soc. Chem. Ind.*, 1903, 69) there is a distinct increase in the amount of free fatty acids in a sewage after passage through a septic tank.

Experiments have also been made on this subject by Rahn (*Centralb. Bakteriol*, 1905, 422), who finds that *Penicillium glaucum* and other penicillia have considerable action on fats, attacking the glycerol and lower fatty acids, though not oleic acid. A motile bacillus, producing a green fluorescent colouring matter, but not identified, had a marked hydrolytic action and decomposed oleic acid. The name "lipobacter" has been proposed by De Kruyff for bacteria which hydrolyse fats.

III. *Use of Chemical Reagents.*—Among the chief accelerators employed in the hydrolysis of oils are sulphuric acid and Twitchell's reagent (benzene- or naphthalene-stearosulphonic acid), while experiments have also been made with hydrochloric acid (*Journ. Soc. Chem. Ind.*, 1903, 67) with fairly satisfactory results, and the use of sulphurous acid, or an alkaline bisulphite as catalyst, has been patented in Germany. To this class belong also the bases, lime, magnesia, zinc oxide, ammonia, soda and potash, though these latter substances differ from the former in that they subsequently combine with the fatty acids liberated to form soaps.

Sulphuric Acid.—The hydrolysing action of concentrated sulphuric acid upon oils and fats has been known since the latter part of the eighteenth century, but was not applied on a practical scale till 1840 when Gwynne patented a process in which sulphuric acid was used to liberate the fatty acids, the latter being subsequently purified by steam distillation.

By this method, sulpho-compounds of the glyceride are first formed, which readily emulsify with water, and, on treatment with steam, liberate fatty acids, the glycerol remaining partly in the form of glycero-sulphuric acid. The process has been investigated by Fremy, Geitel, and more recently by Lewkowitsch (*J. Soc. of Arts*, "Cantor Lectures," 1904, 795 *et seq.*), who has conducted a series of experiments on the hydrolysis of tallow with 4 per cent. of sulphuric acid of varying strengths, containing from 58 to 90 per cent. sulphuric acid, H_2SO_4. Acid of 60 per cent. or less appears to be practically useless as a hydrolysing agent, while with 70 per cent. acid only 47.7 per cent. fatty acids were developed after twenty-two hours' steaming, and with 80 and 85 per cent. acid, the maximum of 89.9 per cent. of fatty acids was only reached after fourteen and fifteen hours' steaming respectively. Using 98 per cent. acid, 93 per cent. of fatty acids were obtained after nine hours' steaming, and after another seven hours, only 0.6 per cent. more fatty acids were produced. Further experiments have shown that dilute sulphuric acid has also scarcely any action on cotton-seed, whale, and rape oils.

According to Lant Carpenter, some 75 per cent. of solid fatty acids may be obtained from tallow by the sulphuric acid process, owing to the conversion of a considerable quantity of oleic acid into isoleic acid (*vide* p. 12), but in the process a considerable proportion of black pitch is obtained. C. Dreymann has recently patented (Eng. Pat. 10,466, 1904) two processes whereby the production of any large amount of hydrocarbons is obviated. In the one case, after saponification with sulphuric acid, the liberated fatty acids are washed with water and treated with an oxide, carbonate, or other acid-fixing body, *e.g.*, sodium carbonate, prior to distillation. In this way the distillate is much clearer than by the ordinary process, and is almost odourless, while the amount of unsaponifiable matter is only about 1.2 per cent. The second method claimed consists in the conversion of the fatty acids into their methyl esters by treatment with methyl alcohol and hydrochloric acid gas, and purification of the esters by steam distillation, the pure esters being subsequently decomposed with superheated steam, in an autoclave, with or without the addition of an oxide, *e.g.*, 0.1 per cent. zinc oxide, to facilitate their decomposition.

Twitchell's Reagent.—In Twitchell's process use is made of the important discovery that aqueous solutions of fatty aromatic sulphuric acids, such as benzene- or naphthalene-stearosulphonic acid, readily dissolve fatty bodies, thereby facilitating their dissociation into fatty acids and glycerol. These compounds are stable at 100° C., and are prepared by treating a mixture of benzene or naphthalene and oleic acid with an excess of sulphuric acid, the following reaction taking place:—

$$C_6H_6 + C_{18}H_{34}O_2 + H_2SO_4 = C_6H_4(SO_3H)C_{18}H_{35}O + H_2O.$$

On boiling the resultant product with water two layers separate, the lower one consisting of a clear aqueous solution of sulphuric acid and whatever benzene-sulphonic acid has been formed, while the upper layer, which is a viscous oil, contains the benzene-stearosulphonic acid. This, after washing first with hydrochloric acid and then rapidly with petroleum ether, and drying at 100° C. is then ready for use; the addition of a small quantity of this reagent to a mixture of fat (previously purified) and water, agitated by boiling with open steam, effects almost complete separation of the fatty acid from glycerol.

The process is generally carried out in two wooden vats, covered with closely fitting lids, furnished with the necessary draw-off cocks, the first vat containing a lead coil and the other a brass steam coil.

In the first vat, the fat or oil is prepared by boiling with 1 or 2 per cent. of sulphuric acid (141° Tw. or 60° B.) for one or two hours and allowed to rest, preferably overnight; by this treatment the fat is deprived of any dirt, lime or other impurity present. After withdrawing the acid liquor, the fat or oil is transferred to the other vat, where it is mixed with one-fifth of its bulk of water (condensed or distilled), and open steam applied. As soon as boiling takes place, the requisite amount of reagent is washed into the vat by the aid of a little hot water through a glass funnel, and the whole is boiled continuously for twelve or even twenty-four hours, until the free fatty acids amount to 85-90 per cent. The amount of reagent used varies with the grade of material, the smaller the amount consistent with efficient results, the better the colour of the finished product; with good material, from 1/2 to 3/4 per cent. is sufficient, but for materials of lower grade proportionately more up to 2 per cent. is required. The reaction appears to proceed better with materials containing a fair quantity of free acidity.

When the process has proceeded sufficiently far, the boiling is stopped and free steam allowed to fill the vat to obviate any discoloration of the fatty acids by contact with the air, whilst the contents of the vat settle.

The settled glycerine water, which should amount in bulk to 50 or 60 per cent. of the fatty matter taken, and have a density of 7-1/2° Tw. (5° B.), is removed to a receptacle for subsequent neutralisation with milk of lime, and, after the separation of sludge, is ready for concentration.

The fatty acids remaining in the vat are boiled with a small quantity (0.05 per cent., or 1/10 of the Twitchell reagent requisite) of commercial barium carbonate, previously mixed with a little water; the boiling may be prolonged twenty or thirty minutes, and at the end of that period the contents of the vat are allowed to rest; the water separated should be neutral to methyl-orange indicator.

It is claimed that fatty acids so treated are not affected by the air, and may be stored in wooden packages.

Hydrochloric Acid.—Lewkowitsch (*Journ. Soc. Chem. Ind.*, 1903, 67) has carried out a number of experiments on the accelerating influence of hydrochloric acid upon the hydrolysis of oils and fats, which show that acid of a specific gravity of 1.16 has a very marked effect on most oils, cocoa-nut, cotton-seed, whale and rape oils, tallow and lard being broken up into fatty acid and glycerol to the extent of some 82-96 per cent. after boiling 100 grams of the oil or fat with 100 c.c. of acid for twenty-four hours. The maximum amount of hydrolysis was attained with cocoa-nut oil, probably owing to its large proportion of the glycerides of volatile fatty acids. Castor oil is abnormal in only undergoing about 20 per cent. hydrolysis, but this is attributed to the different constitution of its fatty acids, and the ready formation of polymerisation products. Experiments were also made as to whether the addition of other catalytic agents aided the action of the hydrochloric acid; mercury, copper sulphate, mercury oxide, zinc, zinc dust, aluminium chloride, nitrobenzene and aniline being tried, in the proportion of 1 per cent. The experiments were made on neutral lard and lard containing 5 per cent. of free fatty acids, but in no case was any appreciable effect produced.

So far this process has not been adopted on the practical scale, its chief drawback being the length of time required for saponification. Undoubtedly the hydrolysis would be greatly facilitated if the oil and acid could be made to form a satisfactory emulsion, but although saponin has been tried for the purpose, no means of attaining this object has yet been devised.

Sulphurous Acid or Bisulphite.—The use of these substances has been patented by Stein, Berge and De Roubaix (Germ. Pat. 61,329), the fat being heated in contact with the reagent for about nine hours at 175°-180° C. under a pressure of some 18 atmospheres, but the process does not appear to be of any considerable importance.

Lime.—The use of lime for the saponification of oils and fats was first adopted on the technical scale for the production of candle-making material, by De Milly in 1831. The insoluble lime soap formed is decomposed by sulphuric acid, and the fatty acids steam distilled.

The amount of lime theoretically necessary to hydrolyse a given quantity of a triglyceride, ignoring for the moment any catalytic influence, can be readily calculated; thus with stearin the reaction may be represented by the equation:—

$$\begin{array}{c} CH_2OOC_{18}H_{35} \\ | \\ 2CHOOC_{18}H_{35} + 3Ca(OH)_2 = 3Ca(OOC_{18}H_{35})_2 + 2CHOH \\ | \\ CH_2OOC_{18}H_{35} \end{array} \quad \begin{array}{c} CH_2OH \\ | \\ \\ | \\ CH_2OH \end{array}$$

stearin — milk of lime — calcium stearate — glycerol

In this instance, since the molecular weight of stearin is 890 and that of milk of lime is 74, it is at once apparent that for every 1,780 parts of stearin, 222 parts of milk of lime or 168 parts of quick-lime, CaO, would be required. It is found in practice, however, that an excess of 3-5 per cent. above the theoretical quantity of lime is necessary to complete the hydrolysis of a fat when carried on in an open vessel at 100°-105° C., but that if the saponification be conducted under pressure in autoclaves the amount of lime necessary to secure almost perfect hydrolysis is reduced to 2-3 per cent. on the fat, the treatment of fats with 3 per cent. of lime under a pressure of 10 atmospheres producing a yield of 95 per cent. of fatty acids in seven hours. The lower the pressure in the autoclave, the lighter will be the colour of the resultant fatty acids.

Magnesia.—It has been proposed to substitute magnesia for lime in the process of saponification under pressure, but comparative experiments with lime and magnesia, using 3 per cent. of lime and 2.7 per cent. of magnesia (*Journ. Soc. Chem. Ind.*, xii., 163), show that saponification by means of magnesia is less complete than with lime, and, moreover, the reaction requires a higher temperature and therefore tends to darken the product.

Zinc Oxide.—The use of zinc oxide as accelerating agent has been suggested by two or three observers. Poullain and Michaud, in 1882, were granted a patent for this process, the quantity of zinc oxide recommended to be added to the oil or fat being 0.2 to 0.5 per cent. Rost, in 1903, obtained a French patent for the saponification of oils and fats by steam under pressure in the presence of finely divided metals or metallic oxides, and specially mentions zinc oxide for the purpose.

It has also been proposed to use zinc oxide in conjunction with lime in the autoclave to obviate to some extent the discoloration of the fatty acids.

Other catalytic agents have been recommended from time to time, including strontianite, lead oxide, caustic baryta, aluminium hydrate, but none of these is of any practical importance.

Soda and Potash.—Unlike the preceding bases, the soaps formed by soda and potash are soluble in water, and constitute the soap of commerce. These reagents are always used in sufficient quantity to combine with the whole of the fatty acids contained in an oil or fat, though doubtless, by the use of considerably smaller quantities, under pressure, complete resolution of the fatty matter into fatty acids and glycerol could be accomplished. They are, by far, the most important saponifying agents from the point of view of the present work, and their practical use is fully described in Chapter V.

CHAPTER III.

RAW MATERIALS USED IN SOAP-MAKING.

Fats and Oils—Waste Fats—Fatty Acids—Less-known Oils and Fats of Limited Use—Various New Fats and Oils Suggested for Soap-making—Rosin—Alkali (Caustic and Carbonated)—Water—Salt—Soap-stock.

Fats and Oils.—All animal and vegetable oils and fats intended for soap-making should be as free as possible from unsaponifiable matter, of a good colour and appearance, and in a sweet, fresh condition. The unsaponifiable matter naturally present as cholesterol, or phytosterol, ranges in the various oils and fats from 0.2 to 2.0 per cent. All oils and fats contain more or less free acidity; but excess of acidity, though it may be due to the decomposition of the glyceride, and does not always denote rancidity, is undesirable in soap-making material. Rancidity of fats and oils is entirely due to oxidation, in addition to free acid, aldehydes and ketones being formed, and it has been proposed to estimate rancidity by determining the amount of these latter produced. It is scarcely necessary to observe how very important it is that the sampling of fats and oils should be efficiently performed, so that the sample submitted to the chemist may be a fairly representative average of the parcel.

In the following short description of the materials used, we give, under each heading, figures for typical samples of the qualities most suitable for soap-making.

Tallows.—Most of the imported tallow comes from America, Australia and New Zealand. South American mutton tallow is usually of good quality; South American beef tallow is possessed of a deep yellow colour and rather strong odour, but makes a bright soap of a good body and texture. North American tallows are, as a general rule, much paler in colour than those of South America, but do not compare with them in consistence. Most of the Australasian tallows are of very uniform quality and much in demand.

Great Britain produces large quantities of tallow which comes into the market as town and country tallow, or home melt. Owing to the increasing demand for edible fat, much of the rough fat is carefully selected, rendered separately, and the product sold for margarine-making. Consequently the melted tallow for soap-making is of secondary importance to the tallow melter.

The following are typical samples of tallow: —

	Saponification Equivalent.	Acidity (as Oleic Acid) Per Cent.	Titre, °C.
Australian mutton	285	0.85	45
Australian mutton	284.4	0.48	48.3
Australian beef	284.2	1.68	43.9
Australian beef	283.6	0.85	42.6
Australian mixed	285.1	3.52	44
Australian mixed	284.6	1.89	43.5
South American mutton	284.5	1.11	47

South American mutton	285	0.90	47.4
South American beef	284.7	0.81	45
South American beef	284	0.94	44
North American mutton	284.3	1.32	44
North American mutton	85	2.18	43.2
North American beef, fine	284.5	1.97	41.5
North American beef, good	283.8	4.30	42
North American ordinary	285.2	5.07	41.75
North American prime city	286	1.01	41.2
Selected English mutton	283.9	1.45	47
Selected English beef	284.2	2.40	44
Home-rendered or country tallow	284.6	5.1	43
Town tallow	285.3	7.4	42.5

Tallow should absorb from 39 to 44 per cent. iodine.

Lard.—Lard is largely imported into this country from the United States of America. The following is a typical sample of American hog's fat offered for soap-making:—

Saponification Equivalent.	Acidity (as Oleic Acid) Per Cent.	Titre, °C.	Refractive Index at 60° C.
286	0.5	37.5	1.4542

Lard should absorb 59 to 63 per cent. iodine.

Cocoa-nut Oil.—The best known qualities are Cochin and Ceylon oils, which are prepared in Cochin (Malabar) or the Philippine Islands and Ceylon respectively.

The dried kernels of the cocoa-nut are exported to various ports in Europe, and the oil obtained comes on the market as Continental Coprah Oil, with the prefix of the particular country or port where it has been crushed, *e.g.*, Belgian, French and Marseilles Coprah Oil. Coprah is also imported into England, and the oil expressed from it is termed English Pressed Coprah.

The following are typical examples from bulk: —

	Saponification Equivalent.	Acidity (as Oleic Acid) Per Cent.	Titre, °C.	Refractive Index at 25° C.
Cochin oil	215.5	1.5	23.5	1.4540
Cochin oil	214.3	2.6	22.1	1.4541
Ceylon oil	214.6	5.47	23	1.4535

Ceylon oil	216	3.95	22.75	1.4535
Belgian coprah	214.2	1.65	23	1.4541
Belgian coprah	215	2.60	22.1	1.4540
French coprah	214.2	6.55	23	1.4535
French coprah	214.8	7.42	22	1.4540
Pressed coprah	215.8	7.45	22.2	1.4542
Pressed coprah	216	9.41	22	1.4555

Cocoa-nut oil should absorb 8.9 to 9.3 per cent. iodine.

Palm-nut Oil.—The kernels of the palm-tree fruit are exported from the west coast of Africa to Europe, and this oil obtained from them. Typical samples of English and Hamburg oils tested:—

Saponification Equivalent.	Acidity (as Oleic Acid) Per Cent.	Titre, °C.	Refractive Index at 25° C.
225	4.4	24	1.4553
227	7.7	23.8	1.4553

Palm-nut oil should absorb 10 to 13 per cent. iodine.

Olive Oil.—The olive is extensively grown in Southern Europe and in portions of Asia and Africa bordering the Mediterranean Sea. The fruit of this tree yields the oil.

The free fatty acid content of olive oil varies very considerably. Very fine oils contain less than 1 per cent. acidity; commercial oils may be graded according to their free acidity, *e.g.*, under 5 per cent., under 10 per cent., etc., and it entirely depends upon the desired price of the resultant soap as to what grade would be used. The following is a typical sample for use in the production of high-class toilet soap:—

Saponification Equivalent.	Acidity (as Oleic Acid) Per Cent.	Titre, °C.	Refractive Index at 15° C.
288	1.8	21	1.4704

Olive oil should absorb 80 to 83 per cent. iodine.

Olive-kernel oil, more correctly termed *Sulphur olive oil*.

The amount of free fatty acids is always high and ranges from 40-70 per cent., and, of course, its glycerol content is proportionately variable. The free acidity increases very rapidly, and is, doubtless, due to the decomposition of the neutral oil by the action of hydrolytic ferment.

A representative sample of a parcel tested:—

Saponification Equivalent.	Acidity (as Oleic Acid) Per Cent.	Refractive Index at 20° C.
298	40.96	1.4666

Palm oil is produced from the fruit of palm trees, which abound along the west coast of Africa. Lagos is the best quality, whilst Camaroons, Bonny, Old Calabar and New Calabar oils are in good request for bleaching purposes.

Analysis of typical samples of crude palm oil has given:—

Saponification Equivalent.	Acidity (as Oleic Acid) Per Cent.	Titre, °C.	Water and Impurities, Per Cent.
278	10.7	45	1.6
280	31.2	44.5	2.8

Palm oil should absorb 51 to 56 per cent. iodine.

In the lower qualities we have examples of the result of hydrolytic decomposition by enzymes, the free acidity often amounting to 70 per cent.

Cotton-seed Oil.—This oil is expressed from the seeds separated from the "wool" of the various kinds of cotton tree largely cultivated in America and Egypt.

In its crude state cotton-seed oil is a dark fluid containing mucilaginous and colouring matter, and is not applicable for soap-making. The following figures are representative of well-refined cotton-seed oils:—

Specific Gravity at 15° C.	Saponification Equivalent.	Acidity (as Oleic Acid) Per Cent.	Titre, °C.	Refractive Index at 20° C.
0.9229	290	0.24	33.6	1.4721
0.924	299	0.39	35	1.4719

Cotton-seed oil should absorb 104 to 110 per cent. iodine.

Cotton-seed Stearine.—The product obtained by pressing the deposit which separates on chilling refined cotton-seed oil.

A typical sample tested:—

Saponification Equivalent.	Acidity (as Oleic Acid) Per Cent.	Titre, °C.
285.1	0.05	38

Arachis Oil.—The earth-nut or ground-nut, from which arachis oil is obtained, is extensively cultivated in North America, India and Western Africa. Large quantities are exported to Marseilles where the oil is expressed. Arachis oil enters largely into the composition of Marseilles White Soaps.

Representative samples of commercial and refined oils tested:—

	Specific Gravity at 15° C.	Saponification Equivalent	Acidity (as Oleic Acid) Per Cent.	Titre, °C.	Refractive Index at 20° C.
Commercial	0.9184	298	2.6	28.6	...
Refined	0.9205	285	0.22	24.0	1.4712

Arachis oil should absorb 90 to 98 per cent. iodine.

Maize Oil.—America (U.S.) produces very large quantities of maize oil.

Typical samples of crude and refined oil gave these figures:—

	Specific Gravity at 15° C.	Saponification Equivalent	Acidity (as Oleic Acid) Per Cent.	Titre, °C.	Refractive Index at 20° C.
Crude	0.9246	294	1.41	15	...
Refined	0.9248	294.1	0.40	17.2	1.4766

Maize oil should absorb 120 to 128 per cent. iodine.

Sesame Oil.—Sesame oil is very largely pressed in Southern France from the seeds of the sesame plant which is cultivated in the Levant, India, Japan and Western Africa.

A fairly representative sample of French expressed oil tested: —

Specific Gravity at 15° C.	Saponification Equivalent	Acidity (as Oleic Acid) Per Cent.	Titre, °C.	Refractive Index at 20° C.
0.9227	295.2	1.84	22.8	1.4731

Sesame oil should absorb 108 to 110 per cent. iodine.

Linseed Oil.—Russia, India, and Argentine Republic are the principal countries which extensively grow the flax plant, from the seeds of which linseed oil is pressed. It is used to a limited extent in soft-soap making.

A good sample gave on analysis:—

Specific Gravity at 15° C.	Saponification Equivalent	Acidity (as Oleic Acid) Per Cent.	Titre, °C.	Refractive Index at 15° C.
0.935	292	1.2	20	1.4840

Linseed oil should absorb 170 to 180 per cent. iodine.

Hemp-seed oil is produced from the seeds of the hemp plant which grows in Russia. This oil is used in soft soap-making, more particularly on the Continent.

A typical sample gave the following figures:—

Specific Gravity at 15° C.	Saponification Equivalent.	Titre, °C.	Iodine No.
0.926	292.6	15.8	143

Sunflower oil is produced largely in Russia.

A specimen tested:—

Specific Gravity at 15° C.	Saponification Equivalent.	Acidity (as Oleic Acid) Per Cent.	Titre, °C.	Iodine No.
0.9259	290.7	0.81	17	126.2

Castor Oil.—The castor oil plant is really a native of India, but it is also cultivated in the United States (Illinois) and Egypt.

A typical commercial sample tested:—

Saponification Equivalent.	Acidity (as Oleic Acid) Per Cent.	Titre, °C.	Iodine No.	Optical Rotation α_D	Refractive Index at 25° C.
310	1.5	2.8	84.1	+4° 50'	1.4787

Fish and Marine Animal Oils.—Various oils of this class have, until recently, entered largely into the composition of soft soaps, but a demand has now arisen for soft soaps made from vegetable oils.

We quote a few typical analyses of these oils:—

	Specific Gravity at 15° C.	Saponification Equivalent.	Acidity (as Oleic Acid) Per Cent.	Titre, °C.	Unsaponifiable Matter Per Cent.
Pale seal oil	0.9252	289	0.947	15.5	0.8
Straw seal oil	0.9231	288	4.77	15.8	1.2
Brown seal oil	0.9253	291	16.38	16.2	1.9
Whale oil	0.9163	297	1.49	16.1	1.8
Dark whale oil	0.9284	303	12.60	21.8	2.4

Japan fish oil	0.9336	296	4.79	26	0.67
Japan fish oil	0.9325	302	10.43	28	1.55
Brown cod oil	0.9260	313	14.91	21.8	1.9
Pure herring oil	0.9353	288	11.39	21.6	1.5
Kipper oil	0.9271	297	5.14	22.7	3.25

Waste Fats.—Under this classification may be included marrow fat, skin greases, bone fats, animal grease, melted stuff from hotel and restaurant refuse, and similar fatty products. The following is a fair typical selection:—

	Saponification Equivalent.	Acidity (as Oleic Acid) Per Cent.	Titre, °C.
Marrow fat	283.3	3.6	38.7
White skin grease	287.2	4.3	36.4
Pale skin grease	286.3	9.87	35.7
Pale bone fat	289.7	8.8	40.7
Brown bone fat	289.1	11.0	41
Brown bone fat	292	20.5	40.2

Animal grease	289.4	38.1	40.4
Melted stuff	286.3	12.8	37.7

The materials in the above class require to be carefully examined for the presence of unsaponifiable matter, lime salts and other impurities.

Fatty Acids.—We have already described the various methods of liberating fatty acids by hydrolysis or saponification.

Under this heading should also be included stearines produced by submitting distilled fat to hydraulic pressure, the distillates from e from unsaponifiable matter, cocoa-nut oleine, a bye-product from the manufacture of edible cocoa-nut butter and consisting largely of free acids, and palm-nut oleine obtained in a similar manner from palm-nut oil.

These are all available for soap-making.

LESS-KNOWN OILS AND FATS OF LIMITED USE.

Shea Butter.—Shea butter is extracted from the kernels of the *Bassia Parkii* and exported from Africa and Eastern India. This fat is somewhat tough and sticky, and the amount of unsaponifiable matter present is sometimes considerable. Samples examined by us gave the following data:—

Saponification Equivalent.	Acidity (as Oleic Acid) Per Cent.	Titre, °C.	Refractive Index at 60° C.
313	8.2	53.2	1.4566
303	7.33	53	1.4558
			1.4471 (F. Acids)

Mowrah-seed Oil.—The mowrah-seed oil now offered for soap-making is derived from the seeds of *Bassia longifolia* and *Bassia latifolia*. It is largely exported from India to Belgium, France and England. The following are the results of some analyses made by us:—

Saponification Equivalent.	Acidity (as Oleic Acid) Per Cent.	Titre, °C.	Refractive Index at 60° C.
291	10	43.4	1.4518
291.5	7.1	42.7	...
291.2	9.9	43.8	...
292	11.26	40.5	...

Chinese vegetable tallow is the name given to the fat which is found coating the seeds of the "tallow tree" (*Stillingia sebifera*) which is indigenous to China and has been introduced to India where it flourishes. The following is a typical sample:—

Saponification Equivalent	Acidity Per Cent.	Titre, °C.
280.2	5.24	52.5

The seeds of the "tallow tree" yield an oil (stillingia oil) having drying properties.

Borneo Tallow.—The kernels of several species of *Hopea* (or *Dipterocarpus*), which flourish in the Malayan Archipelago, yield a fat known locally as Tangawang fat. This fat is moulded (by means of bamboo canes) into the form of rolls about 3 inches thick, and exported to Europe as Borneo Tallow.

A sample tested by one of us gave the following data:—

Saponification Equivalent.	Acidity (as Oleic Acid) Per Cent.	Titre, °C.
292	36	50.8

Kapok oil is produced from a tree which is extensively grown in the East and West Indies. The Dutch have placed it on the market and the figures given by Henriques (*Chem. Zeit.*, 17, 1283) and Philippe (*Monit. Scient.*, 1902, 730), although varying somewhat, show the oil to be similar to cotton-seed oil.

VARIOUS NEW FATS AND OILS SUGGESTED FOR SOAP-MAKING.

Carapa or *Andiroba oil*, derived from the seeds of a tree (*Carapa Guianensis*) grown in West Indies and tropical America, has been suggested as suitable for soap-making.

Deering (*Imperial Institute Journ.*, 1898, 313) gives the following figures:—

Saponification Equivalent.	Acidity Per Cent.	Melting Point of Fatty Acids, °C.
287	12	89

Another observer (*Rev. Chem. Ind.*, 13, 116) gives the setting point of the fatty acids as 56.4° C.

Candle-nut oil obtained from the seeds of a tree flourishing in India and also the South Sea Islands.

The following figures have been published:—

Saponification Equivalent.[1]	Titre, °C.	Iodine No.	Observers.	References.
299-304.9	13	136.3-139.3	De Negri	*Chem. Centr.*, 1898, p. 493.
291	...	163.7	Lewkowitsch	*Chem. Revue*, 1901, p. 156.
296	12.5	152.8	Kassler	*Farben-Zeitung*, 1903, p. 359.

---

[1] Saponification Equivalents calculated by us from saponification value.

Curcas oil is produced in Portugal from the seeds of the "purging nut tree," which is similar to the castor oil plant, and is cultivated in Cape Verde Islands and other Portuguese Colonies.

The following data have been observed:—

Saponification Equivalent.	Titre, °C.	Iodine No.	Observers.	References.
291.4	0.36	99.5	Archbut	*J. S. C. Ind.*, 1898, p. 1010.
290.3	4.46	98.3	Lewkowitsch	*Chem. Revue*, 1898, p. 211.
283.1	0.68	107.9	Klein	*Zeits. angew. Chem.*, 1898, p. 1012.

The titre is quoted by Lewkowitsch as 28.6° C.

Goa butter or *Kokum butter* is a solid fat obtained from the seeds of *Garcinia indica*, which flourishes in India and the East Indies. Crossley and Le Sueur (*Journ. Soc. Chem. Industry*, 1898, p. 993) during an investigation of Indian oils obtained these results:—

Saponification Equivalent.	Acidity Per Cent.	Iodine No.
300	7.1	34.2

Safflower oil is extracted from the seeds of the *Carthamus tinctorius*, which, although indigenous to India and the East

Indies, is extensively cultivated in Southern Russia (Saratowa) and German East Africa. Its use has been suggested for soft-soap making. The following figures have been published:—

Saponification Equivalent.	Titre, °C.	Iodine No.	Observers.	References.
Average of Twelve Samples	295.5	141.29	Crossley and Le Sueur	*J. S. C. Ind.*, 1898, p. 992; *J. S. C. Ind.*, 1900, p. 104.
	287.1	141.6	Shukoff	*Chem. Revue*, 1901, p. 250.
	289.2	130	Tylaikow	*Chem. Revue*, 1902, p. 106.
	293.7	142.2	Fendler	*Chem. Zeitung*, 1904, p. 867.

Maripa fat is obtained from the kernels of a palm tree flourishing in the West Indies, but, doubtless, the commercial fat is obtained from other trees of the same family. It resembles cocoa-nut oil and gives the following figures:—

Saponification Equivalent.	Iodine No.	Melting Point of Fatty Acids, °C.	Observer.	Reference.
217	9.49	25	Bassière	*J. S. C. Ind.*, 1903, p. 1137.

Niam fat, obtained from the seeds of *Lophira alata*, which are found extensively in the Soudan. The fat, as prepared by natives, has been examined by Lewkowitsch, and more recently Edie has published the results of an analysis. The figures are as follows:—

Saponification Equivalent.	Titre, °C.	Iodine No.	Observers.	References.
295.1	78.12	42.5	Lewkowitsch	*J. S. C. Ind.*, 1907, p. 1266.
287.7	75.3		Edïe.	*Quart. J. Inst. Comm. Research in Tropics.*

Cohune-nut oil is produced from the nuts of the cohune palm, which flourishes in British Honduras. This oil closely resembles cocoa-nut and palm-nut oils and is stated to saponify readily and yield a soap free from odour. The following figures, obtained in the Laboratory of the Imperial Institute, are recorded in the official *Bulletin*, 1903, p. 25: —

Saponification Equivalent.	Iodine No.	Melting Point of Fatty Acids, °C.
253.9-255.3	12.9-13.6	27-30

Mafoureira or *Mafura tallow* from the nuts of the mafoureira tree, which grows wild in Portuguese East Africa. The following figures are published:—

Saponification Equivalent.	Titre, °C.	Iodine No.	References.
253.8	44-48	46.14	De Negri and Fabris, *Annal. del Lab. Chim. Delle Gabelle*, 1891-2, p. 271.
	Acidity (as Oleic Acid) Per Cent.		
232.8-233.7	21.26	47.8-55.8	*Bulletin Imp. Inst.*, 1903, p. 27.

Pongam oil, obtained from the beans of the pongam tree, which flourishes in East India, has been suggested as available for the soap industry, but the unsaponifiable matter present would militate against its use. Lewkowitsch (*Analyst*, 1903, pp. 342-44) quotes these results:—

	Saponification Equivalent.	Iodine No.	Acidity, Per Cent.	Unsaponifiable, Per Cent.	
Oil extracted in laboratory	315	94	3.05		9.22
Indian specimen	306	89.4	0.5		6.96

Margosa oil is obtained from the seeds of *Melia azedarach*, a tree which is found in most parts of India and Burma.

Lewkowitsch (*Analyst*, 1903, pp. 342-344) gives these figures:—

Saponification Equivalent.	Iodine No.	Titre, °C.
284.9	69.6	42

Dika fat or *Wild Mango oil* is obtained from the seed kernels of various kinds of *Irvingia* by boiling with water. Lemarié (*Bulletin Imp. Inst.*, 1903, p. 206) states that this fat is used in the place of cocoa-nut oil in the manufacture of soap. Lewkowitsch (*Analyst*, 1905, p. 395) examined a large sample of dika fat obtained from seeds of *Irvingia bateri* (South Nigeria) and gives the following data:—

Saponification Equivalent.	Iodine No.	Titre, °C.	Unsaponifiable, Per Cent.
229.4	5.2	34.8	0.73

Baobab-seed Oil.—Balland (*Journ. Pharm. Chem.*, 1904, p. 529, abstracted in *Journ. Soc. Chem. Ind.*, 1905, p. 34) states that the natives of Madagascar extract, by means of boiling water, from the seeds of the baobab tree, a whitish solid oil, free from rancidity, and possessed of an odour similar to Tunisian olive oil. He suggests that it may, with advantage, replace cocoa-nut oil in soap manufacture.

Persimmon-seed Oil.—Lane (*J. S. C. Ind.*, 1905, p. 390) gives constants for this oil which he describes as semi-drying, of brownish yellow colour, and having taste and odour like pea-nut (arachis) oil. The following are taken from Lane's figures:—

Saponification Equivalent.	Iodine No.	Titre, °C.
298.4	115.6	20.2

Wheat oil, extracted from the wheat germ by means of solvents, has been suggested as applicable for soap-making (H. Snyder, abstr. *J. S. C. Ind.*, 1905, p. 1074). The following figures have been published: —

Saponification Equivalent.	Acidity, Per Cent.	Iodine No.	Titre, °C.	Observers.	References.
306	5.65	115.17	29.7	De Negri.	*Chem. Zeit.*, 1898 (abstr. *J. S. C.*, 1898, p. 1155).
297	20	115.64	...	Frankforter & Harding	*J. Amer. C. Soc.*, 1899, 758-769 (abstr. in *J. S. C. I.*, 1899, p. 1030).

Tangkallah fat, from the seeds of a tree growing in Java and the neighbouring islands, is suitable for soap-making. Schroeder (*Arch. Pharm.*, 1905, 635-640, abstracted in *J. S. C. Ind.*, 1906, p. 128) gives these values:—

Saponification Equivalent.	Acidity, Per Cent.	Iodine No.	Unsaponifiable, Per Cent.
209	1.67	2.28	1.44

It is a hard fat, nearly white, possessing neither taste nor characteristic odour and solidifying at about 27° C.

Oil of Inoy-kernel.—(*Bulletin Imp. Inst.*, 1906, p. 201). The seeds of Poga oleosa from West Africa yield on extraction an oil which gives the figures quoted below, and is suggested as a soap-maker's material:—

Saponification Equivalent.	Iodine No.	Titre, °C.
304	89.75	22

ROSIN.

Rosin is the residuum remaining after distillation of spirits of turpentine from the crude oleo-resin exuded by several species of the pine, which abound in America, particularly in North Carolina, and also flourish in France and Spain. The gigantic forests of the United States consist principally of the long-leaved pine, *Pinus palustris (Australis)*, whilst the French and Spanish oleo-resin is chiefly obtained from *Pinus pinaster*, which is largely cultivated.

Rosin is a brittle, tasteless, transparent substance having a smooth shining fracture and melting at about 135° C. (275° F.). The American variety possesses a characteristic aromatic odour, which is lacking in those from France and Spain. It is graded by samples taken out of the top of every barrel, and cut into 7/8 of an inch cubes, which must be uniform in size—the shade of colour of the cube determines its grade and value.

The grades are as follows:—

W. W. (Water white.)
W. G. (Window glass.)
N. (Extra pale.)
M. (Pale.)
K. (Low pale.)
I. (Good No. 1.)
H. (No. 1.)
G. (Low No. 1.)
F. (Good No. 2.)
E. (No. 2.)
D. (Good strain.)
C. (Strain.)
B. (Common strain.)
A. (Common.)

Unsaponifiable matter is present in rosin in varying amounts.

Below are a few typical figures taken from a large number of collated determinations:—

	Saponification Equivalent.	Total Acid No.	Free Acid No.	Iodine No.
American W. W.	330.5	169.7	119.1	126.9
American N.	312.3	179.6	161.4	137.8
French	320.5	175	168	120.7
Spanish	313.4	179	160	129.8

ALKALI (CAUSTIC AND CARBONATED).

The manufacture of alkali was at one time carried on in conjunction with soap-making, but of late years it has become more general for the soap manufacturer to buy his caustic soda or carbonated alkali from the alkali-maker.

Although there are some alkali-makers who invoice caustic soda and soda ash in terms of actual percentage of sodium oxide (Na_2O), it is the trade custom to buy and sell on what is known as the English degree, which is about 1 per cent. higher than this.

The English degree is a survival of the time when the atomic weight of sodium was believed to be twenty-four instead of twenty-three, and, since the error on 76 per cent. Na_2O due to this amounts to about 1 per cent., may be obtained by adding this figure to the sodium oxide really present.

Caustic soda (sodium hydrate) comes into commerce in a liquid form as 90° Tw. (and even as high as 106° Tw.), and other degrees of dilution, and also in a solid form in various grades as 60°, 70°, 76-77°, 77-78°. These degrees represent the percentage of sodium oxide (Na_2O) present plus the 1 per cent. The highest grade, containing as it does more available caustic soda and less impurities, is much more advantageous in use.

Carbonate of soda or *soda ash*, 58°, also termed "light ash," and "refined alkali". This is a commercially pure sodium carbonate containing about 0.5 per cent. salt (NaCl). The 58° represents the English degrees and corresponds to 99 per cent. sodium carbonate (Na_2CO_3).

Soda ash, 48°, sometimes called "caustic soda ash," often contains besides carbonate of soda, 4 per cent. caustic soda (sodium hydrate), and 10 per cent. salt (sodium chloride), together with water and impurities.

The 48 degrees refers to the amount of alkali present in terms of sodium oxide (Na_2O), but expressed as English degrees.

Caustic potash (potassium hydrate) is offered as a liquid of 50-52° B. (98-103° Tw.) strength, and also in solid form as 75-80° and 88-92°. The degrees in the latter case refer to the percentage of potassium hydrate (KHO) actually present.

Carbonate of Potash.—The standard for refined carbonate of potash is 90-92 per cent. of actual potassium carbonate (K_2CO_3) present, although it can be obtained testing 95-98 per cent.

OTHER MATERIALS.

Water.—Water intended for use in soap-making should be as soft as possible. If the water supply is hard, it should be treated chemically; the softening agents may be lime and soda ash together, soda ash alone, or caustic soda. There are many excellent plants in vogue for water softening, which are based on similar principles and merely vary in mechanical arrangement. The advantages accruing from the softening of hard water intended for steam-raising are sufficiently established and need not be detailed here.

Salt (sodium chloride or common salt, NaCl) is a very important material to the soap-maker, and is obtainable in a very pure state.

Brine, or a saturated solution of salt, is very convenient in soap-making, and, if the salt used is pure, will contain 26.4 per cent. sodium chloride and have a density of 41.6° Tw. (24.8° B.).

The presence of sulphates alters the density, and of course the sodium chloride content.

Salt produced during the recovery of glycerine from the spent lyes often contains sulphates, and the density of the brine made from this salt ranges higher than 42° Tw. (25° B.).

Soapstock.—This substance is largely imported from America, where it is produced from the dark-coloured residue, termed mucilage, obtained from the refining of crude cotton-seed oil. Mucilage consists of cotton-seed oil soap, together with the colouring and resinous principles separated during the treatment of the crude oil. The colouring matter is removed by boiling the mucilage with water and graining well with salt; this treatment is repeated several times until the product is free from excess of colour, when it is converted into soap and a nigre settled out from it.

Soapstock is sold on a fatty acid basis; the colour is variable.

CHAPTER IV.

BLEACHING AND TREATMENT OF RAW MATERIALS INTENDED FOR SOAP-MAKING.

Palm Oil—Cotton-seed Oil—Cotton-seed "Foots"—Vegetable Oils—Animal Fats—Bone Fat—Rosin.

Having described the most important and interesting oils and fats used or suggested for use in the manufacture of soap, let us now consider briefly the methods of bleaching and treating the raw materials, prior to their transference to the soap-pan.

Crude Palm Oil.—Of the various methods suggested for bleaching palm oil, the bichromate process originated by Watts is undoubtedly the best. The reaction may be expressed by the following equation, though in practice it is necessary to use twice the amount of acid required by theory:—

$K_2Cr_2O_7 + 14HCl = 2KCl + Cr_2Cl_6 + 7H_2O + 6Cl$.

$6Cl + 3H_2O = 6HCl + 3O$.

The palm oil, freed from solid impurities by melting and subsidence, is placed in the bleaching tank, and washed with water containing a little hydrochloric acid. Having allowed it to rest, and drawn off the liquor and sediment (chiefly sand), the palm oil is ready for treatment with the bleaching reagent, which consists of potassium bichromate and commercial muriatic acid. For every ton of oil, 22 to 28 lb. potassium bichromate and 45 to 60 lb. acid will be found sufficient to produce a good bleached oil.

The best procedure is to act upon the colouring matter of the oil three successive times, using in the first two treatments one-third of the average of the figures just given, and in the final treatment an appropriate quantity which can be easily gauged by the appearance of a cooled sample of the oil.

The potassium bichromate is dissolved in hot water and added to the crude palm oil, previously heated to 125° F. (52° C.), the requisite amount of muriatic acid being then run in and the whole well agitated by means of air. The bright red colour of the oil gradually changes to dark brown, and soon becomes green. The action having proceeded for a few minutes, agitation is stopped, and, after allowing to settle, the green liquor is withdrawn.

When sufficiently bleached the oil is finally washed (without further heating) with hot water (which may contain salt), to remove the last traces of chrome liquor.

If the above operation is carried out carefully, the colouring matter will be completely oxidised.

It is important, however, that the temperature should not be allowed to rise above 130° F. (54° C.) during the bleaching of palm oil, otherwise the resultant oil on saponification is apt to yield a soap of a "foxy" colour. The bleached oil retains the characteristic violet odour of the original oil.

It has been suggested to use dilute sulphuric acid, or a mixture of this and common salt, in the place of muriatic acid in the above process.

Crude Cotton-seed Oil.—The deep colouring matter of crude cotton-seed oil, together with the mucilaginous and resinous principles, are removed by refining with caustic soda lye.

The chief aim of the refiner is to remove these impurities without saponifying any of the neutral oil. The percentage of free fatty acids in the oil will determine the quantity of caustic lye required, which must only be sufficient to remove this acidity.

Having determined the amount of free acidity, the quantity of caustic soda lye necessary to neutralise it is diluted with water to 12° or 15° Tw. (8° or 10° B.), and the refining process carried out in three stages. The oil is placed in a suitable tank and heated by means of a closed steam coil to 100° F. (38° C.), a third of the necessary weak caustic soda lye added in a fine stream or by means of a sprinkler, and the whole well agitated with a mechanical agitator or by blowing a current of air through a pipe laid on the bottom of the tank.

Prolonged agitation with air has a tendency to oxidise the oil, which increases its specific gravity and refractive index, and will be found in the soap-pan to produce a reddish soap. As the treatment proceeds, the temperature may be carefully raised, by means of the steam coil, to 120° F. (49° C.).

The first treatment having proceeded fifteen minutes, the contents of the tank are allowed to rest; the settling should be prolonged as much as possible, say overnight, to allow the impurities to precipitate well, and carry down the least amount of entangled oil. Having withdrawn these coloured "foots," the second portion of the weak caustic soda solution is agitated with the partially refined oil, and, when the latter is sufficiently treated, it is allowed to rest and the settled coloured liquor drawn off as before. The oil is now ready for the final treatment, which is performed in the same manner as the two previous ones. On settling, a clear yellow oil separates.

If desired, the oil may be brightened and filtered, after refining to produce a marketable article, but if it is being refined for own use in the soap-house, this may be omitted.

The residue or "foots" produced during the refining of crude cotton-seed oil, known in the trade as "mucilage," may be converted into "soapstock" as mentioned in the preceding chapter, or decomposed by a mineral acid and made into "black grease" ready for distillation by superheated steam.

Vegetable Oils.—The other vegetable oils come to the soap-maker's hand in a refined condition; occasionally, however, it is desirable to remove a portion of the free fatty acids, which treatment also causes the colouring matter to be preciptated. This is effected by bringing the oil and a weak solution of caustic lye into intimate contact. Cocoa-nut oil is often treated in this manner. Sometimes it is only necessary to well agitate the oil with 1-1/2 per cent. of its weight of a 12° Tw. (8° B.) solution of caustic soda and allow to settle. The foots are utilised in the soap-pan.

Animal Fats.—Tallows are often greatly improved by the above alkaline treatment at 165° F. (73° C.). It is one of the best methods and possesses advantages over acid processes—the caustic soda removes the free acid and bodies of aldehyde nature, which are most probably the result of oxidation or polymerisation, whereas the neutral fat is not attacked, and further, the alkaline foots can be used in the production of soap.

Bone fat often contains calcium (lime) salts, which are very objectionable substances in a soap-pan. These impurities must be removed by a treatment with hydrochloric or sulphuric acid. The former acid is preferable, as the lime salt formed is readily soluble and easily removed. The fat is agitated with a weak solution of acid in a lead-lined tank by blowing in steam, and when the treatment is complete and the waste liquor withdrawn, the last traces of acid are well washed out of the liquid fat with hot water.

Rosin.—Several methods have been suggested for bleaching rosin; in some instances the constitution of the rosin is altered, and in others the cost is too great or the process impracticable.

The aim of these processes must necessarily be the elimination of the colouring matter without altering the original properties of the substance. This is best carried out by converting the rosin into a resinate of soda by boiling it with a solution of either caustic soda or carbonated alkali. The process is commenced by heating 37 cwt. of 17° Tw. (11° B.) caustic soda lye, and adding 20 cwt. of rosin, broken into pieces, and continuing the boiling until all the resinate is homogeneous, when an addition of 1-1/2 cwt. of salt is made and the boiling prolonged a little. On resting, the coloured liquor rises to the surface of the resinate, and may be siphoned off (or pumped away through a skimmer pipe) and the resinate further washed with water containing a little salt.

The treatment with carbonated alkali is performed in a similar manner. A solution, consisting of 2-3/4 cwt. of soda ash (58°), in about four times its weight of water, is heated and 20 cwt. of rosin, broken into small pieces, added. The whole is heated by means of the open steam coil, and care must be taken to avoid boiling over. Owing to the liberation of CO_2 gas, frothing takes place. A large number of patents have been granted for the preparation of resinate of soda, and many methods devised to obviate the boiling over. Some suggest mixing the rosin and soda ash (or only a portion of the soda ash) prior to dissolving in water; others saponify in a boiler connected with a trap which returns the resinate to the pan and allows the carbonic-acid gas to escape or to be collected.

With due precaution the method can be easily worked in open vessels, and, using the above proportions, there will be sufficient uncombined rosin remaining to allow the resultant product to be pumped into the soap with which it is intended to intermix it, where it will be finally saponified thoroughly.

The salt required, which, in the example given, would be 1-1/2 cwt., may be added to the solution prior to the addition of rosin or sprinkled in towards the finish of the boiling. When the whole has been sufficiently boiled and allowed to rest, the liquor containing the colouring matter will float over the resinate, and, after removal, may be replaced by another washing.

Many other methods have been suggested for the bleaching, refining and treatment of materials intended for saponification, but the above practical processes are successfully employed.

All fats and oils after being melted by the aid of steam must be allowed to thoroughly settle, and the condensed water and impurities withdrawn through a trap arrangement for collecting the fatty matter. The molten settled fatty materials *en route* to the soap-pan should be passed through sieves sufficiently fine to free them from suspended matter.

CHAPTER V.

SOAP-MAKING.

Classification of Soaps—Direct Combination of Fatty Acids with Alkali—Cold Process Soaps—Saponification under Increased or Diminished Pressure—Soft Soap—Marine Soap—Hydrated Soaps, Smooth and Marbled—Pasting or Saponification—Graining Out—Boiling on Strength—Fitting—Curd Soaps—Curd Mottled—Blue and Grey Mottled Soaps—Milling Base—Yellow Household Soaps—Resting of Pans and Settling of Soap—Utilisation of Nigres—Transparent Soaps—Saponifying Mineral Oil—Electrical Production of Soap.

Soaps are generally divided into two classes and designated "hard," and "soft," the former being the soda salts, and the latter potash salts, of the fatty acids contained in the material used.

According to their methods of manufacture, soaps may, however, be more conveniently classified, thus:—

(A) Direct combination of fatty acids with alkali.

(B) Treatment of fat with definite amount of alkali and no separation of waste lye.

(C) Treatment of fat with indefinite amount of alkali and no separation of waste lye.

(D) Treatment of fat with indefinite amount of alkali and separation of waste lye.

(A) *Direct Combination of Fatty Acids with Alkali.*—This method consists in the complete saturation of fatty acids with alkali, and permits of the use of the deglycerised products mentioned in chapter ii., section 2, and of carbonated alkalies or caustic soda or potash. Fatty acids are readily saponified with caustic soda or caustic potash of all strengths.

The saponification by means of carbonated alkali may be performed in an open vat containing a steam coil, or in a pan provided with a removable agitator.

It is usual to take soda ash (58°), amounting to 19 per cent. of the weight of fatty acids to be saponified, and dissolve it in water by the aid of steam until the density of the solution is 53° Tw. (30° B.); then bring to the boil, and, whilst boiling, add the molten fatty acids slowly, but not continuously.

Combination takes place immediately with evolution of carbonic acid gas, which causes the contents of the vat or pan to swell, and frequently to boil over. The use of the agitator, or the cessation of the flow of fatty acids, will sometimes tend to prevent the boiling over. It is imperative that the steam should not be checked but boiling continued as vigorously as possible until all the alkali has been absorbed and the gas driven off.

The use of air to replace steam in expelling the carbonic acid gas has been patented (Fr. Pat. 333,974, 1903).

A better method of procedure, however, is to commence with a solution of 64° Tw. (35° B.) density, made from half the requisite soda ash (9-1/2 per cent.), and when this amount of alkali has all been taken up by the fatty acids (which have been added gradually and with continuous boiling), the remaining quantity of soda ash is added in a dry state, being sprinkled over each further addition of fatty acid.

This allows the process to be more easily controlled and boiling over is avoided.

It is essential that the boiling by steam should be well maintained throughout the process until all carbonic acid gas has been thoroughly expelled; when that point is reached, the steam may be lessened and the contents of the vat or pan gently boiled "on strength" with a little caustic lye until it ceases to absorb caustic alkali, the soap being finished in the manner described under (D).

It is extremely difficult to prevent discoloration of fatty acids, hence the products of saponification in this way do not compare favourably in appearance with those produced from the original neutral oil or fat.

(B) *Treatment of Fat with Definite Amount of Alkali and no Separation of Waste Lye.*—Cold-process soap is a type of this class, and its method of production is based upon the characteristic property which the glycerides of the lower fatty acids (members of the cocoa-nut-oil class) possess of readily combining with a strong caustic soda solution at a low temperature, and evolving sufficient heat to complete the saponification.

Sometimes tallow, lard, cotton-seed oil, palm oil and even castor oil are used in admixture with cocoa-nut oil. The process for such soap is the same as when cocoa-nut oil is employed alone, with the slight alteration in temperature necessary to render the fats liquid, and the amount of caustic lye required will be less. Soaps made of these blends closely resemble, in appearance, milled toilet soaps. In such mixtures the glycerides of the lower fatty acids commence the saponification, and by means of the heat generated induce the other materials, which alone would saponify with difficulty or only with the application of heat, to follow suit.

It is necessary to use high grade materials; the oils and fats should be free from excess of acidity, to which many of the defects of cold-process soaps may be traced. Owing to the rapidity with which free acidity is neutralised by caustic soda, granules of soap are formed, which in the presence of strong caustic lye are "grained out" and difficult to remove without increasing the heat; the soap will thus tend to become thick and gritty and sometimes discoloured.

The caustic lye should be made from the purest caustic soda, containing as little carbonate as possible; the water used for dissolving or diluting the caustic soda should be soft (*i.e.*, free from calcium and magnesium salts), and all the materials carefully freed from particles of dirt and fibre by straining.

The temperature, which, of course, must vary with the season, should be as low as is consistent with fluidity, and for cocoa-nut oil alone may be 75° F. (24° C.), but in mixtures containing tallow 100° to 120° F. (38° to 49° C.).

The process is generally carried out as follows:—

The fluid cocoa-nut oil is stirred in a suitable vessel with half its weight of 71.4° Tw. (38° B.) caustic soda lye at the same temperature, and, when thoroughly mixed, the pan is covered and allowed to rest. It is imperative that the oils and fats and caustic lye should be intimately incorporated or emulsified. The agitating may be done mechanically, there being several machines specially constructed for the purpose. In one of the latest designs the caustic lye is delivered through a pipe which rotates with the stirring gear, and the whole is driven by means of a motor.

The agitation being complete, chemical action takes place with the generation of heat, and finally results in the saponification of the fats.

At first the contents of the pan are thin, but in a few hours they become a solid mass. As the process advances the edges of the soap become more transparent, and when the transparency has extended to the whole mass, the soap is ready, after perfuming, to be framed and crutched.

The admixture of a little caustic potash with the caustic soda greatly improves the appearance of the resultant product, which is smoother and milder.

The glycerine liberated during the saponification is retained in the soap.

Although it is possible, with care, to produce neutral soaps of good appearance and firm touch by this method, cold-process soaps are very liable to contain both free alkali and unsaponified fat, and have now fallen considerably into disrepute.

Saponification under Increased or Diminished Pressure.— Soaps made by boiling fats and oils, under pressure and *in vacuo*, with the exact quantity of caustic soda necessary for complete combination, belong also to this class. Amongst the many attempts which have at various times been made to shorten the process of soap-making may be mentioned Haywood's Patent No. 759, 1901, and Jourdan's French Patent No. 339,154, 1903.

In the former, saponification is carried out in a steam-jacketed vacuum chamber provided with an elaborate arrangement of stirrers; in the other process fat is allowed to fall in a thin stream into the amount of lye required for saponification, previously placed in the saponification vessel, which is provided with stirring gear.

When the quantities have been added, steam is admitted and saponification proceeds.

(C) *Treatment of Fat with Indefinite Amount of Alkali and no Separation of Waste Lye.*—*Soft soap* is representative of this class. The vegetable fluid oils (linseed, olive, cottonseed, maize) are for the most part used in making this soap, though occasionally bone fats and tallow are employed. Rosin is sometimes added, the proportion ranging, according to the grade of soap required, from 5 to 15 per cent. of the fatty matter.

The Soft Soap Manufacturers' Convention of Holland stipulate that the materials used in soft-soap making must not contain more than 5 per cent. rosin; it is also interesting to note that a patent has been granted (Eng. Pat. 17,278, 1900) for the manufacture of soft soap from material containing 50 per cent. rosin.

Fish or marine animal oils—whale, seal, etc., once largely used as raw material for soft soap, have been superseded by vegetable oils.

The materials must be varied according to the season; during hot weather, more body with a less tendency to separate is given by the introduction of oils and fats richer in stearine; these materials also induce "figging".

The most important material, however, is the caustic potash lye which should average 40° Tw. (24° B.), *i.e.*, if a weak solution is used to commence saponification, a stronger lye must be afterwards employed to avoid excess of water in the soap, and these average 40° Tw. (24° B.). The potash lye must contain carbonates, which help to give transparency to the resultant soap. If the lye is somewhat deficient in carbonates, they may be added in the form of a solution of refined pearl ash (potassium carbonate).

Caustic soda lye is sometimes admixed, to the extent of one-fourth, with potash lye to keep the soap firmer during hot weather, but it requires great care, as a slight excess of soda gives soft soap a bad appearance and a tendency to separate.

The process is commenced by running fatty matter and weak potash lyes into the pan or copper, and boiling together, whilst the introduction of oil and potash lye is continued.

The saponification commences when an emulsion forms, and the lye is then run in more quickly to prevent the mass thickening.

Having added sufficient "strength" for complete saponification, the boiling is continued until the soap becomes clear.

The condition of the soap is judged by observing the behaviour of a small sample taken from the pan and dropped on glass or iron. If the soap is satisfactory it will set firm, have a short texture and slightly opaque edge, and be quite clear when held towards the light. If the cooled sample draws out in threads, there is an excess of water present. If an opaque edge appears and vanishes, the soap requires more lye. If the sample is turbid and somewhat white, the soap is too alkaline and needs more oil.

The glycerine liberated during saponification is contained in the soap and no doubt plays a part in the production of transparency.

Hydrated soaps, both smooth and marbled, are included in this classification, but are *soda* soaps. Soap made from cocoa-nut oil and palm-kernel oil will admit of the incorporation of large quantities of a solution of either salt, carbonate of soda, or silicate of soda, without separation, and will retain its firmness. These materials are, therefore, particularly adapted for the manufacture of marine soaps, which often contain as much as 80 per cent. of water, and, being soluble in brine, are capable of use in sea-water. For the same reason, cocoa-nut oil enters largely into the constitution of hydrated soaps, but the desired yield or grade of soap allows of a variation in the choice of materials. Whilst marine soap, for example, is usually made from cocoa-nut oil or palm-kernel oil only, a charge of 2/3 cocoa-nut oil and 1/3 tallow, or even 2/3 tallow and 1/3 cocoa-nut oil, will produce a paste which can carry the solutions of silicate, carbonate, and salt without separation, and yield a smooth, firm soap.

The fatty materials, carefully strained and freed from particles of dirt and fibre, are boiled with weak caustic soda lye until combination has taken place. Saponification being complete, the solution of salt is added, then the carbonate of soda solution, and finally the silicate of soda solution, after which the soap is boiled. When thoroughly mixed, steam is shut off, and the soap is ready for framing.

The marbled hydrated soap is made from cocoa-nut oil or a mixture of palm-kernel oil and cocoa-nut oil with the aid of caustic soda lye 32-1/2° Tw. (20° B.). As soon as saponification is complete, the brine and carbonate of soda solution are added, and the pan allowed to rest.

The soap is then carefully tasted as to its suitability for marbling by taking samples and mixing with the colouring solution (ultramarine mixed with water or silicate of soda solution). If the sample becomes blue throughout, the soap is too alkaline; if the colour is precipitated, the soap is deficient in alkali. The right point has been reached when the marbling is distributed evenly. Having thus ascertained the condition of the pan, and corrected it if necessary, the colour, mixed in water or in silicate of soda solution, is added and the soap framed.

(D) *Treatment of Fat with Indefinite Amount of Alkali and Separation of Waste Lye.*—This is the most general method of soap-making. The various operations are:—

(*a*) Pasting or saponification.
(*b*) Graining out or separation.
(*c*) Boiling on strength.

And in the case of milling soap base and household soaps,

(*d*) Fitting.

(*a*) *Pasting or Saponification.*—The melted fats and oils are introduced into the soap-pan and boiled by means of open steam with a caustic soda lye 14° to 23.5° Tw. (10° to 15° B.). Whether the fatty matters and alkali are run into the pan simultaneously or separately is immaterial, provided the alkali is not added in sufficient excess to retard the union.

The commencement of the saponification is denoted by the formation of an emulsion. Sometimes it is difficult to start the saponification; the presence of soap will often assist this by emulsifying the fat and thus bringing it into intimate contact with the caustic soda solution.

When the action has started, caustic soda lye of a greater density, 29° to 33° Tw. (18° to 20° B.), is frequently added, with continued boiling, in small quantities as long as it is being absorbed, which is ascertained by taking out samples from time to time and examining them.

There should be no greasiness in the sample, but when pressed between finger and thumb it must be firm and dry.

Boiling is continued until the faint caustic taste on applying the cooled sample to the tongue is permanent, when it is ready for "graining out". The pasty mass now consists of the soda salts of the fat (as imperfect soap, probably containing emulsified diglycerides and monoglycerides), together with water, in which is dissolved the glycerine formed by the union of the liberated glyceryl radicle from the fat with the hydroxyl radicle of the caustic soda, and any slight excess of caustic soda and carbonates. The object of the next operation is to separate this water (spent lye) from the soap.

(*b*) *Graining Out or Separation.*—This is brought about by the use of common salt, in a dry form or in solution as brine, or by caustic soda lye. Whilst the soap is boiling, the salt is spread uniformly over its surface, or brine 40° Tw. (24° B.) is run in, and the whole well boiled together. The soap must be thoroughly boiled after each addition of salt, and care taken that too large a quantity is not added at once.

As the soap is gradually thrown out of solution, it loses its smooth transparent appearance, and becomes opaque and granular.

When a sample, taken out on a wooden trowel, consists of distinct grains of soap and a liquid portion, which will easily separate, sufficient salt or brine has been added; the boiling is stopped and the spent lye allowed to settle out, whilst the soap remains on the surface as a more or less thick mass.

The separated spent lye consists of a solution of common salt, glycerine, and alkaline salts; the preparation of crude glycerine therefrom is considered in chapter ix.

The degree of separation of water (spent lye) depends upon the amount of precipitant used. The aim is to obtain a maximum amount of spent lye separated by the use of a minimum quantity of salt.

The amount of salt required for "graining out" varies with the raw material used. A tallow soap is the most easily grained, more salt is required for cotton-seed oil soap, whereas soaps made from cocoa-nut and palm-kernel oils require very large amounts of salt to grain out thoroughly. Owing to the solubility in weak brine of these latter soaps, it is preferable to grain them with caustic soda lye. This is effected by adding, during boiling, sufficient caustic lye (32-1/2° Tw., 20° B.) to produce the separation of the granules of soap. The whole is allowed to rest; the separated half-spent lye is withdrawn and may be used for the pasting of fresh materials.

After the removal of the settled lye, the grained mass is boiled with sufficient water to dissolve the grain and make it smooth ("close" it), and is now ready for the next operation of "boiling on strength".

(*c*) *Boiling on Strength or Clear Boiling.*—This is the most important operation and is often termed "making the soap". The object is to harden the soap and to ensure complete saponification.

Caustic soda lye (32-1/2° Tw., 20° B.) is gradually added until the soap is again opened or grained, and boiling continued by the use of the dry steam coil. As soon as the caustic soda lye is absorbed, another portion is slowly added, and this is continued until the caustic soda or "strength" remains permanent and the soapy mass, refusing to absorb more, is thrown out of solution and grained. The granular mass will boil steadily, and the boiling should be prolonged, as the last traces of neutral oil are difficult to completely saturate with alkali. Thorough saponification takes place gradually, and the operation cannot be hurried; special care has to be bestowed upon this operation to effect the complete combination of fat and alkali.

After resting for several hours, half-spent lye settles to the bottom of the pan. In the case of yellow soaps or milling bases the settled lye is removed to a suitable receptacle and reserved for use in the saponification of other material, and the soap is then ready for the final operation of "fitting".

(*d*) *Fitting.*—If the operations just described have been properly performed, the fitting should present no difficulty. The soap is boiled with open steam, and water added until the desired degree of closing is attained. As the water is thoroughly intermixed throughout the mass the thick paste gradually becomes reduced to a smooth, thin consistence. Samples are tested from time to time as to their behaviour in dropping off a hot trowel held sideways; the thin layer should drop off in two or three flakes and leave the surface of the trowel clean and dry. The soap is then in a condition to allow the impurities to gravitate. According to the required soap, the fit may be "coarse" ("open") when the flakes drop off the trowel readily, or "fine" ("close") when the flakes only leave the trowel with difficulty.

If the dilution with water has been allowed to proceed too far, and too fine a fit is produced, which would be denoted by the layer of soap not leaving the trowel, a little caustic lye or brine may be very carefully added and the whole well boiled until the desired condition is obtained.

A good pressure of steam is now applied to the pan, causing the contents to swell as high as possible, this greatly facilitating the settling of impurities; steam is then turned off, the pan covered, and the boil allowed to rest for several days.

The art of fitting consists in leaving the contents of the pan in such a condition that, on standing, all the impurities precipitate, and the settled soap, containing the correct amount of water, is clear and bright.

The above is a general practical outline of the ordinary soap-boiling process. It may be modified or slightly altered according to the fancy of the individual soap-maker or the particular material it is desired to use. Fats and oils not only vary in the amount of alkali they absorb during saponification, but also differ in the strength of the alkali they require. Tallow and palm oil require lye of a density of 15° to 18° Tw. (10° to 12° B.), but cocoa-nut oil alone would not saponify unless the lye was more concentrated, 33° to 42° Tw. (20° to 25° B.). Cotton-seed oil requires weak lyes for saponification, and, being difficult to saponify alone even with prolonged boiling, is generally mixed with animal fat.

When fats are mixed together, however, their varying alkali requirements become modified, and once the saponification is begun with weak lye, other materials are induced to take up alkali of a strength with which alone they would not combine.

It is considered the best procedure to commence the pasting or saponification with weak lye.

In order to economise tank space, it is the general practice to store strong caustic lye (60° to 70° Tw., 33° to 37° B.) and to dilute it as it is being added to the soap-pan by the simultaneous addition of water.

Many manufacturers give all their soap a "brine wash" to remove the last traces of glycerine and free the soap from carbonates. This operation takes place prior to "fitting"; sufficient water is added to the boiling soap to "close" it and then brine is run in to "grain" it.

After resting, the liquor is withdrawn.

Having described the necessary operations in general, we will now consider their application to the preparation of various kinds of hard soap.

Curd Soaps.—Tallow is largely used in the manufacture of white curd soaps, but cocoa-nut oil sometimes enters into their composition.

The first three operations above described, *viz.*, pasting, graining out, and boiling on strength, are proceeded with; the clear boiling by means of a closed steam coil is continued until the "head" is boiled out and the soap is free from froth. A sample taken and cooled should be hard. Boiling is then stopped, and, after covering, the pan is allowed to rest for eight to ten hours, when the soap is ready for filling into frames, where it is crutched until perfectly smooth.

Curd mottled is usually made from melted kitchen stuff and bone grease.

Its preparation is substantially the same as for curd soap, but the clear boiling is not carried so far. The art of curd mottled soap-making lies in the boiling. If boiled too long the mottling will not form properly, and, on the other hand, insufficient boiling will cause the soap to contain an excess of entangled lye. Having boiled it to its correct concentration the pan is allowed to rest about two hours, after which the soap is ready for framing, which should be done expeditiously and the frames covered up.

Some lye, containing the impurities from the fats used, remains in the interstices of the curd, unable to sink, and as the soap cools it is enclosed and forms the mottling. The mottling may, therefore, be considered as a crystallisation of the soap, in which the impurity forms the colour.

Blue and Grey Mottled Soaps.—These are silicated or liquored soaps in which the natural mottling, due to the impure materials used in the early days of soap-making, is imitated by artificial mottling, and are, consequently, entirely different to curd mottled soaps.

The materials employed in making mottled soap comprise bleached palm oil, tallow, bone fat, cocoa-nut oil, palm-kernel oil, cotton-seed oil, and, in some instances, rosin.

The choice of a charge will naturally depend upon the cost; the property of absorbing a large amount of liquor, which is characteristic of soaps made from cocoa-nut oil and palm-kernel oil, is taken advantage of, as are also the physical properties of the various fats and oils, with a view to the crystallisation of the resultant soap and the development of the mottle. The fat is saponified, grained and boiled on strength, as previously described. After withdrawing the half-spent lye, the soap is just closed by boiling with water, and is then ready for the silicate or other saline additions.

Soap intended to be liquored with silicate of soda should be distinctly strong in free alkali; the crystalline nature of the soap is increased thereby, and the mottled effect intensified. Some makers, however, fit the soap coarsely and allow a nigre to deposit; then, after removing the nigre, or transferring the settled soap to another copper, containing scraps of mottled soap, get the soap into a condition for mottling, and add the silicate of soda solution. To every 1 cwt. of soap, 28 lb. of silicate of soda solution, 32-1/2° Tw. (20° B.) is added, whilst boiling; the strength of the silicate solution, however, will depend upon the proportion of cocoa-nut oil and palm-kernel oil present in the charge. Many soap-makers use 20° Tw. (13° B.) (cold) silicate solution, whilst others prefer 140° Tw. (59.5° B.), with the gradual addition of water to the soap, kept boiling, until the product is in the correct mottling condition, and others, again, use bleach liquor, soda crystals, pearl ash, and salt, together with silicate solution.

Considerable skill and experience is necessary to discern when the soap acquires the correct mottling state. It should drop off the spatula in large thick flakes, take considerable time to set, and the surface should not be glossy.

When this mottling condition has been obtained, the colouring matter, which would be ultramarine for the blue mottled and manganese dioxide for the grey mottled soap (3-4 lb. ultramarine or 1-3 lb. manganese dioxide being sufficient for 1 ton of soap), is mixed with a little water and added to the boiling soap—the boiling is continued until all is thoroughly amalgamated, and when the steam is shut off the contents of the pan are ready for cleansing.

Mottled soap is run into wooden frames, which, when full, are covered over and allowed to cool very gradually. On cooling slowly, large crystals are produced which result in a distinct bold mottle; if the cooling is too rapid, a small crystal is obtained and the mottle is not distributed, resulting in either a small mottle, or no mottle at all, and merely a general coloration. In fact, the entire art of mottling soap consists in properly balancing the saline solutions and colouring matter, so that the latter is properly distributed throughout the soap, and does not either separate in coloured masses at the bottom of the frame, or uniformly colour the whole mass.

A sample of the soap should test 45 per cent. fatty acids, and the amount of salt would range from 1/2 to 1 per cent.

Some of the English mottled soaps, especially those made from materials which give a yellow-coloured ground, are bleached by soaking in brine, or pickling in brine containing 2 per cent. of bleach liquor. The resultant soap has a white ground and is firm. The bleach liquor may be made by mixing 1 cwt. bleaching powder with 10 cwts. of soda ash solution (15° Tw., 10° B.), allowing to settle, and using the clear liquid, or by mixing 2 parts soda ash solution with 1 part of bleaching powder solution, both solutions being 30° Tw. (18.8° B.).

Milling-base.—The materials generally used are tallows and cocoa-nut oils of the finest quality. The tallow is thoroughly saponified first, and the graining is performed by the aid of caustic soda lye in preference to salt. The half-spent lyes are withdrawn, and the cocoa-nut oil added to the pan. This is saponified, and when the saponification is complete, "boiling-on-strength" is proceeded with. Special care should be devoted to the "boiling-on-strength" operation—its value in good soap-making cannot be over-rated—and perfect saponification must be ensured. The half-spent lyes are allowed to deposit during the night, and the soap must be carefully examined next morning to ascertain if any alkali has been absorbed. If the caustic taste is permanent the strengthening operation is complete, but should any caustic have been absorbed, further addition of alkali must be made and the boiling continued. These remarks apply equally to all soaps.

The soap, when ready, is fitted.

Bleached palm oil, olive oil, castor oil and lard are also employed in the production of special milling soap bases, a palm oil soap being specially suitable for the production of a violet-scented toilet soap.

Yellow Household Soaps. (a) Bar Soaps.—These are made from tallow with an admixture of from 15-25 per cent. rosin. The best quality is known in the South and West of England as Primrose Soap, but is designated in the North of England by such names as Golden Pale, Imperial Pale, Gold Medal Pale, etc. Tallow alone produces a very hard soap of inferior lathering qualities; but rosin combines with alkali to form a soft body, which, although not a soap in the strict sense of the term, is readily soluble in water, and in admixture with the durable tallow soap renders it more soluble in water and thereby increases its lathering properties.

The rosin may be added to the soap-pan after a previous partial saponification with soda ash, and removal of colouring matter, and finally saponified with caustic soda lye, or, as is more generally adopted, as a rosin change. The pan is opened with caustic soda lye and saturation of the rosin takes place rapidly; when completely saponified it is grained with salt, and the coloured lye allowed to deposit and finally withdrawn.

The four operations already detailed apply to this soap.

Cheaper pale soaps may be made from lower grades of tallow and rosin and are generally silicated.

(*b*) *Tablet or Washer Type.*—A demand has arisen for soap of free lathering qualities, which has become very popular for general household use. This soap is usually made from a mixture of cotton-seed oil, tallow, and cocoa-nut oil, with a varying amount of rosin. The tallow yields firmness and durability whilst the other constituents all assist in the more ready production of a copious lather.

As to what amount of rosin can be used to yield a finished soap of sufficient body and satisfactory colour, this naturally depends upon the grade of raw material at the soap-makers' disposal. Those fats and oils which yield firm soaps, will, of course, allow a greater proportion of rosin to be incorporated with them than materials producing soaps of less body. Rosin imparts softness to a soap, and also colour.

This is a fitted soap and full details of manufacture have already been given.

Cheaper soaps are produced from lower grade materials hardened with alkaline solutions.

Resting of Pans and Settling of Soap.—The fitted soap is allowed to settle from four to six days. The period allowed for resting is influenced, however, not only by the size of the boil, and the season, but also by the composition of the soap, for if the base has been made from firm stock it is liable to cool quicker than a soap produced from soft-bodied materials.

On subsidence, the contents of the pan will have divided into the following:—

First. On top, a thin crust of soap, with perhaps a little light coloured fob, which is returned to the pan after the removal of the good soap.

Second. The good settled soap, testing 62-63 per cent. fatty acids. The subject of removing and treatment of this layer is fully dealt with in the next chapter.

Third. A layer of darker weak soap, termed "nigre," which on an average tests 33 per cent. fatty acids, and, according to the particular fit employed, will amount to from 15-20 per cent. of the total quantity of soap in the pan.

The quantity of nigre may vary not only with the amount of water added during finishing, but is also influenced by the amount of caustic alkali remaining in the soap paste prior to fitting. If the free caustic alkali-content is high, the soap will require a large amount of water to attain the desired fit. This water renders the caustic into a lye sufficiently weak to dissolve a quantity of soap, consequently, as the "nigre" is a weak solution of soap together with any excess of alkali (caustic or carbonate) and salt which gravitates during the settling, the quantity is increased.

Fourth. A solution containing alkaline salts, mostly carbonates and chlorides, with a little caustic.

The amount of the layer is very variable, and doubtless, under certain physical conditions, this liquor has separated from the nigre.

Utilisation of Nigres.—The nigres are boiled and the liquor separated by graining with salt. Nigre may be utilised in various ways.

(1) It may be used several times with new materials. This particularly refers to soaps of the "Washer" type. The colour of the nigre will determine the number of times it can be employed.

(2) It may be incorporated with a soap of a lower grade than the one from which it was obtained. In this case a system is generally adopted; for example, soap of the best quality is made in a clean pan, the nigre remaining is worked up with fresh material for soap of the next quality, the nigre from that boil, in its turn, is admixed with a charge to produce a batch of third quality, and the deposited nigre from this is again used for a fourth quality soap—the nigre obtained from this latter boil would probably be transferred into the cheapened "washer" or perhaps if it was dark in colour into the brown soap-pan.

(3) The nigre may be fitted and produce a soap similar to the original soap from which it was deposited. It is advisable to saponify a little fat with it.

(4) Nigres from several boils of the same kind of soap can be collected, boiled, and fitted. The settled portion may be incorporated with a new charging to keep the resultant soap uniform in colour—unless this is done, the difference in colour between boils from new materials alone, and those

containing nigre, is very noticeable. The nigre settled from this fitted nigre boil would be utilised in brown soap.

(5) According to its colour, and consistence, a nigre may be suitable for the production of disinfectant, or cold-water soaps.

(6) Nigre may be bleached by treatment with a 20 per cent. solution of stannous chloride—1 cwt. of this solution (previously heated) is sufficient to bleach 20 tons of nigre.

Transparent Soaps.—The production of transparent soaps has recently been fully studied, from a theoretical point of view, by Richardson (*J. Amer. Chem. Soc.*, 1908, pp. 414-20), who concludes that the function of substances inducing transparency, is to produce a jelly and retard crystallisation.

The old-fashioned transparent soap is prepared by dissolving, previously dried, genuine yellow soap in alcohol, and allowing the insoluble saline impurities to be deposited and removed. The alcoholic soap solution is then placed in a distillation apparatus, or the pan containing the solution is attached by means of a still head to a condenser, and the alcohol distilled, condensed and regained. The remaining liquid soap, which may be coloured and perfumed, is run into frames and allowed to solidify.

The resultant mass is somewhat turbid, but after storage in a room at 95° F. (35° C.) for several months, becomes transparent.

The formation of the transparency is sometimes assisted and hastened by the addition of glycerine or a solution of cane-sugar.

A patent has been granted to A. Ruch (Fr. Pat. 327,293, 1902) for the manufacture of transparent glycerine soap by heating in a closed vessel fatty acids together with the requisite quantity of alcoholic caustic soda solution necessary for saponification, and cooling the resultant soap. It is also proposed to add sugar solution.

Cheaper qualities of transparent soaps are made by the cold process with or without the aid of alcohol and castor oil, and with the assistance of glycerine or cane-sugar.

With the continual demand for cheaper production, sugar solution has gradually, in conjunction with castor oil, which produces transparency, superseded the use of alcohol and glycerine.

For a small batch, 56 lb. Cochin cocoa-nut oil and 56 lb. sweet edible tallow may be taken, melted at 130° F. (54° C.), and carefully strained into a small steam-jacketed pan. It is imperative that the materials should be of the highest quality and perfectly clean. Twenty-three lb. of pure glycerine and 56 lb. of bright caustic soda solution made from high grade caustic and having a density of 72° Tw. (38° B.) are crutched into the fat; the alcohol, which would be 45 lb. in this example, is then added. The whole must be most intimately incorporated, and the pan covered and allowed to rest for one hour or one and a half hours. Saponification should ensue.

To produce a transparent glycerine soap with the aid of castor oil, and with or without the use of alcohol, the following is the procedure:—

Cochin cocoa-nut oil, sweet edible tallow, and castor oil, of each 56 lb. are taken, warmed to 130° F. (54° C.), and carefully strained into the jacketed pan. If it is desired to use glycerine and cane sugar solution, and no alcohol, the glycerine (25 lb.) is now stirred into the fats together with the requisite (83 lb.) caustic soda solution 72° Tw. (38° B.). If it is intended to use alcohol and sugar, and no glycerine, the latter is replaced by 47 lb. of alcohol, and added after the incorporation of the caustic soda lye.

The whole being thoroughly crutched, the pan is covered and saponification allowed to proceed for one hour or one and a half hours. Should the saponification for some reason be retarded, a little steam may be very cautiously admitted to the jacket of the pan, the mass well crutched until the reaction commences, and the whole allowed to rest the specified time.

Whilst saponification is proceeding, the "sugar solution" is prepared by dissolving 50 lb. cane sugar in 50 lb. water, at 168° F. (76° C.), to which may be added 5 lb. soda crystals, and any necessary colouring matter. The water used for this solution should be as soft as possible, as hard water is liable to produce opaque streaks of lime soap.

It is absolutely necessary before proceeding further to ensure that saponification is complete. A greasy, soft feel and the presence of "strength" (caustic) would denote incomplete saponification—this can only be remedied by further heating and crutching. Deficiency of caustic alkali should also be avoided, and, if more lye is required, great care must be exercised in its addition.

Saponification being completed, the sugar solution is carefully and gradually crutched into the soap; when the contents of the pan have become a homogeneous and syrupy mass, the crutching is discontinued, and the pan is covered for one hour. The heat of the soap in the pan should not exceed 170° F. (77° C.).

Having rested the necessary period, the soap will have a slight froth on the surface, but will be clear underneath and appear dark. Samples may now be withdrawn, cooled, and examined prior to framing. If the process has been successfully performed the soap will be firm and transparent, of uniform colour, and possess only a faintly alkaline taste.

If the sample be firm but opaque, more sugar solution is required; this should be added very carefully whilst crutching, an excess being specially guarded against. If the sample be soft, although transparent, and the alkaline taste not too pronounced, the soap evidently contains an excess of water, which may be remedied by the addition of a small quantity of soda ash; too much soda ash (carbonates) must be avoided, lest it should produce efflorescence.

Having examined the soap and found it to be correct, or having remedied its defects, the soap in the pan is allowed to cool to 145° F. (63° C.) and perfume added. The soap is now quickly filled into narrow frames and allowed to cool rapidly.

The blocks of soap should not be stripped until quite cold throughout, and they should be allowed to stand open for a while before slabbing. When freshly cut into tablets, the soap may appear somewhat turbid, but the brightness comes with the exposure it will receive prior to stamping and wrapping.

Saponifying Mineral Oil.—This sounds somewhat incongruous, as mineral oil is entirely unsaponifiable. Most of the suggestions for this purpose consist of the incorporation of mineral oil, or mineral oil emulsified by aid of Quillaia bark, with a cocoa-nut oil soap, and in all these instances the hydrocarbon merely exists in suspension.

G. Reale (Fr. Pat. 321,510, 1902), however, proposes to heat mineral oil together with spermaceti and strong alkali, and states that he transforms the hydrocarbons into alcohols, and these, absorbing oxygen, become fatty acids, which are converted into soap by means of the alkali.

In this connection may be quoted the interesting work of Zelinsky (*Russ. Phys. Chem. Ges. Zeits. Angew. Chem.*, 1903, 37). He obtained substances, by acting with carbon dioxide upon magnesia compounds of chlorinated fractions of petroleum, which when decomposed by dilute sulphuric acid, yielded various organic acids. One of these acids on heating with glycerine formed tri-octin, which had the properties of a fat.

Dr. Engler, in confirmation of the theory of the animal origin of some petroleums, obtained what might be described as petroleum (for it contained almost all the hydrocarbons present in the natural mineral oil) by distilling animal fats and oils under pressure.

Electrical Production of Soap.—Attempts have been made to produce soap electrically by Messrs. Nodon, Brettonneau and Shee (Eng. Pat. 22,129, 1897), and also by Messrs. Merry and Noble (Eng. Pat. 2,372, 1900).

In the former patent, a mixture of soda-lye and fat is agitated by electricity at a temperature of 194°-212° F. (90°-100° C.), while in the latter caustic alkali is electrolytically produced from brine, and deposited on wire-netting in the presence of fat, which is thereby saponified.

CHAPTER VI.

TREATMENT OF SETTLED SOAP.

Cleansing—Crutching—Liquoring of Soaps—Filling—Neutralising, Colouring and Perfuming—Disinfectant Soaps—Framing—Slabbing—Barring—Open and Close Piling—Drying—Stamping—Cooling.

Cleansing.—After completion of saponification, and allowing the contents of the pan to settle into the various layers, as described in the preceding chapter, the actual soap, forming the second layer, is now transferred to the frames, this being generally termed "cleansing" the soap. The thin crust or layer at the top of the pan is gently removed, and the soap may be either ladled out and conveyed to the frames, or withdrawn by the aid of a pump from above the nigre through a skimmer (Fig. 1), and pipe, attached by means of a swivel joint (Fig. 2) (which allows the skimmer pipe to be raised or lowered at will by means of a winch, Fig. 3), to a pipe fitted in the side of the pan as fully shown in Fig. 4, or the removal may be performed by gravitation through some mechanical device from the side of the copper.

Fig. 1.—Skimmer, with flange for attachment to skimmer-pipe.

Every precaution is taken to avoid the presence of nigre in the soap being cleansed.

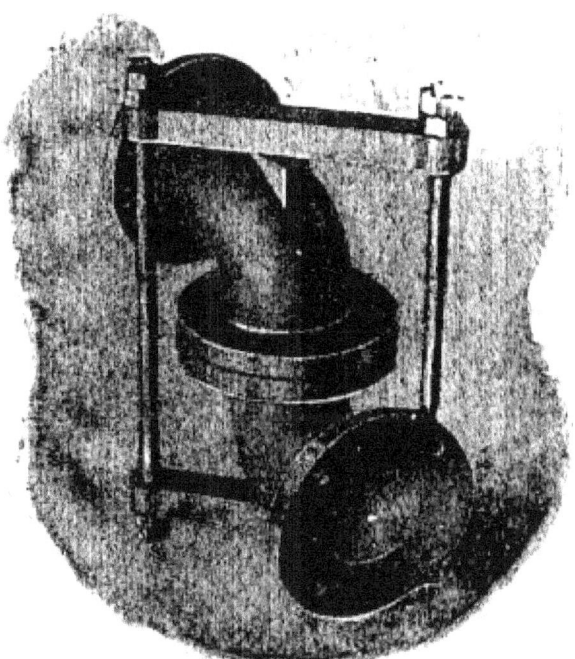

Fig. 2.—Swivel-joint.

The temperature at which soap may be cleansed depends on the particular grade—soaps requiring to be liquored should not be cleansed too hot or a separation will take place, 150° F. (66° C.) may be taken as a suitable temperature for this class of soap; in the case of firm soaps, such as milling base, where cooling is liable to take place in the pan (and thus affect the yield), the temperature may be 165°-170° F. (74°-77° C.). This latter class of soap is generally run direct to the frames and crutched by hand, or, to save manual labour, it may be run into a power-driven crutching pan (neutralising material being added if necessary) and stirred a few times before framing.

Fig. 3.—Winch.

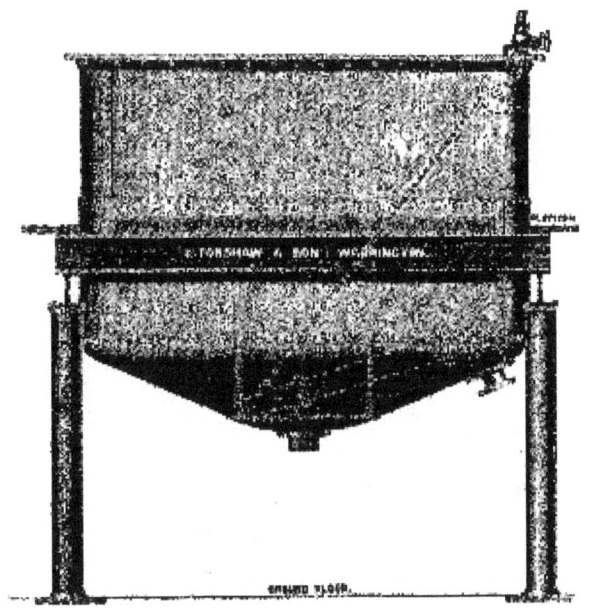

Fig. 4.—Soap-boiling pan, showing skimmer pipe, swivel and winch.

Fig. 5.—Hand crutch.

Fig. 6.—Mechanical crutcher.

Crutching.—This consists of stirring the hot soap in the frames by hand crutches (Fig. 5) until the temperature is sufficiently lowered and the soap begins to assume a "ropiness". Crutching may also be performed mechanically. There are various types of mechanical crutchers, stationary and travelling. They may be cylindrical pans, jacketed or otherwise, in the centre of which is rotated an agitator, consisting of a vertical or horizontal shaft carrying several blades (Fig. 6) or the agitator may take the form of an Archimedean screw working in a cylinder (Fig. 7).

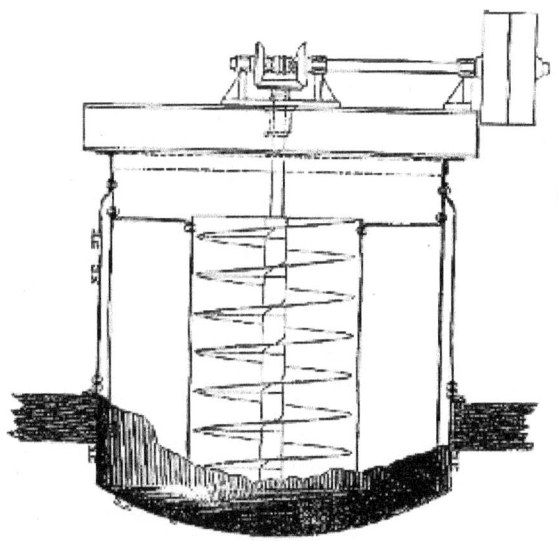

Fig. 7.—Mechanical crutcher.

The kind of soap to be crutched, whether thin or stiff, will determine the most suitable type for the purpose. The former class includes "washer" soap which is generally neutralised, and coloured and perfumed, if necessary, in these crutching pans, and in that case they are merely used for mixing the liquids with the hot soap prior to its passage along wooden spouts (Fig. 8) provided with outlets over the frames, in which the crutching is continued by hand. In the case of stiff soaps requiring complete incorporation of liquor, the screw type is preferable, the soap being forced upwards by the screw, and descending between the cylinder and the sides of the pan, while the reverse action can also be brought into play. The completion of crutching is indicated by the smoothness and stiffness of the soap when moved with a trowel, and a portion taken out at this point and cooled should present a rounded appearance. When well mixed the resultant product is emptied directly into wheel-frames placed underneath the outlet of the pan. It is important that the blades or worm of the agitating gear be covered with soap to avoid the occlusion of air and to prevent the soap becoming soft and spongy.

Fig. 8.—Wooden soap spout.

Liquoring of Soaps.—This consists of the addition of various alkaline solutions to soap to produce different qualities, and is best performed in the crutching machines, although it is in some instances carried out in the frames. In the history of soap-making a large number and variety of substances have been suggested for the purpose of accomplishing some real or supposed desirable effect when added to soap. Many of these have had only a very short existence, and others have gradually fallen out of use.

Amongst the more practical additions most frequently adopted may be mentioned carbonate of soda, silicate of soda, and pearl ash (impure carbonate of potash). The carbonate of soda may be used in the form of "soda crystals," which, containing 62.9 per cent. of water, dissolves in its own water of crystallisation on heating, and is in that manner added to the hot soap. In the case of weak-bodied soap, this addition gives firmness and tends to increase the detergent qualities.

The soda carbonate may also be added to soap as a solution of soda ash (58° alkali) either concentrated, 62° Tw. (34° B.), or of various strengths from 25° Tw. (16° B.) upwards. This solution stiffens and hardens soap, and the addition, which must not be excessive, or efflorescence will occur, is generally made at a temperature of 140° F. (60° C.). Care should always be taken in the choice of solutions for liquoring. Strong soda ash solution with a firm soap will result in a brittle product, whereas the texture of a weak soap would be greatly improved by such addition.

A slight addition of a weak solution of pearl ash, 4°-8° Tw. (2.7-5.4° B.), improves the appearance of many soaps intended for household purposes.

For yellow soaps, containing a low percentage of fatty acids, solutions of silicate of soda of varying strengths are generally used.

It is always advisable to have a test sample made with the soap to ascertain what proportion and what strength of sodium silicate solution is best suited for the grade of soap it is desired to produce. It is important that the soap to be "silicated" should be distinctly alkaline (*i.e.*, have a distinct caustic taste), or the resultant soap is liable to become like stone with age. The alkaline silicate of soda (140° Tw., 59.5° B.) is the quality most convenient for yellow soaps; this may be diluted to the desired gravity by boiling with water. For a reduction of 3-4 per cent. fatty acids content, a solution of 6° Tw. (4° B.) (boiling) is most suitable, and if the reduction desired is greater, the density of the silicate solution should be increased; for example, to effect a reduction of 20 per cent. fatty acids content, a solution of 18° Tw. (12° B.) (boiling) would probably be found to answer.

In some instances 140° Tw. (59.5° B.) silicate may be added; experiment alone will demonstrate the amount which can be satisfactorily incorporated without the soap becoming "open," but 1/10 of the quantity of soap taken is practically a limit, and it will be found that the temperature should be low; the same quantity of silicate at different temperatures does not produce the same result. Various other strengths of sodium silicate are employed, depending upon the composition and body of the soap base—neutral silicate 75° Tw. (39.4° B.) also finds favour with some soap-makers. Mixtures of soda crystals or soda ash solution with silicate of soda solution are used for a certain grade of soap, which is crutched until smooth and stiff. Glauber's salt (sodium sulphate) produces a good smooth surface when added to soap, but, owing to its tendency to effloresce more quickly than soda carbonate, it is not so much used as formerly.

Common salt sometimes forms an ingredient in liquoring mixtures. Potassium chloride and potassium silicate find a limited use for intermixing with soft soaps.

It will be readily understood that hard and fast rules cannot be laid down for "liquoring" soap, and the correct solution to be employed can only be ascertained by experiment and experience, but the above suggestions will prove useful as a guide towards good results. A smooth, firm soap of clear, bright, glossy appearance is what should be aimed at.

Filling.—Some low-grade soaps contain filling, which serves no useful purpose beyond the addition of weight. Talc is the most frequently used article of this description. It consists of hydrated silicate of magnesium and, when finely ground, is white and greasy to the touch. The addition of this substance to the hot soap is made by suspending it in silicate of soda solution.

Whatever filling material is used, it is important that the appearance of the soap should not be materially altered.

Neutralising, Colouring and Perfuming.—The free caustic alkali in soap, intended for toilet or laundry purposes, is usually neutralized during the cleansing, although some soap manufacturers prefer to accomplish this during the milling operation. Various materials have been recommended for the purpose, those in most general use being sodium bicarbonate, boric acid, cocoa-nut oil, stearic acid, and oleic acid.

The best method is the addition of an exact quantity of sodium bicarbonate (acid sodium carbonate), which converts the caustic alkali into carbonate. The reaction may be expressed by the equation:—

$$\underset{\text{Caustic soda}}{NaOH} + \underset{\text{Bicarbonate of soda}}{NaHCO_3} = \underset{\text{Carbonate of soda}}{Na_2CO_3} + \underset{\text{Water}}{H_2O}$$

Boric acid in aqueous or glycerine solutions, and borax (biborate of soda) are sometimes used, but care is necessary in employing these substances, as any excess is liable to decompose the soap.

The addition of cocoa-nut oil is unsatisfactory, the great objection being that complete saponification is difficult to ensure, and, further, there is always the liability of rancidity developing. Stearic and oleic acids are more suitable for the purpose, but oleic acid has the disadvantage that oleates are very liable to go rancid.

A large number of other substances have been proposed, and in many instances patented, for neutralising the free caustic alkali. Among these may be mentioned—Alder Wright's method of using an ammoniacal salt, the acid radicle of which neutralises the caustic alkali, ammonia being liberated; the use of sodium and potassium bibasic phosphate (Eng. Pat. 25,357, 1899); a substance formed by treating albumen with formalin (Eng. Pat., 8,582, 1900); wheat glutenin "albuminoses" (albumen after acid or alkaline treatment); malt extract; and egg, milk, or vegetable albumen.

The colouring matter used may be of either vegetable or coal-tar origin, and is dissolved in the most suitable medium (lye, water, or fat). The older types of colouring matter—such as cadmium yellow, ochres, vermilion, umbers—have been superseded.

In the production of washer household soaps, a small quantity of perfume is sometimes added.

Disinfectant Soaps.—To the soap base, which must be strong to taste, is added from 3 to 4 per cent. of coal-tar derivatives, such as carbolic acid, cresylic acid, creosote, naphthalene, or compounds containing carbolic acid and its homologues. The incorporation is made in the crutching pan, and further crutching may be given by hand in the frames.

Framing.—The object of framing is to allow the soap to solidify into blocks. The frames intended for mottled soaps, which require slow cooling, are constructed of wood, often with a well in the base to allow excess of lye to accumulate—for other soaps, iron frames are in general use. The frame manufactured by H. D. Morgan of Liverpool is shown in Fig. 9.

As soon as the frame is filled, or as soon as the crutching in the frame is finished, the soap is smoothed by means of a trowel, leaving in the centre a heap which slopes towards the sides. Next day the top of the soap is straightened or flattened with a wooden mallet, this treatment assisting in the consolidation.

Fig. 9.—Soap frame.

Fig. 10.—Slabbing machine.

The length of time the soap should remain in frames is dependent on the quality, quantity, and season or temperature, and varies usually from three to seven days. When the requisite period has elapsed, the sides and ends of the frames are removed, and there remains a solid block of soap weighing from 10 to 15 cwt. according to the size of frame used. The blocks, after scraping and trimming, are ready for cutting into slabs.

Slabbing.—This may be done mechanically by pushing the block of soap through a framework containing pianoforte wires fixed at equi-distances (Fig. 10, which shows a machine designed by E. Forshaw & Son, Ltd.), or the soap may be out by hand by pulling a looped wire through the mass horizontally along lines previously scribed, or, for a standard sized slab, the wire may be a fixture in a box-like arrangement, which is passed along the top of the soap, and the distance of the wire from the top of the box will be the thickness of the slab (Fig. 11).

Fig. 11.—Banjo slabber.

All tallow soaps should be slabbed whilst still warm, cut into bars, and open-piled immediately; if this type of soap is cold when slabbed its appearance will be very much altered.

Barring.—The slabs are out transversely into bars by means of the looped wire, or more usually by a machine (Fig. 12), the lower framework of which, containing wires, is drawn through the soap placed on the base-board; the framework is raised, and the bars fall upon the shelf, ready for transference into piles. It has long been the custom in England to cut bars of soap 15 inches long, and weighing 3 lb. each, or 37-1/2 bars of soap to the cwt., but in recent years a demand has arisen for bars of so many various weights that it must be sometimes a difficult matter to know what sizes to stock.

In another type of barring machine, portions of the slab, previously cut to size, are pushed against a framework carrying wires, and the bars slide along a table ready for handling (Fig. 13).

In cutting machines, through which "washer" household soap is being passed, the bar is pushed at right angles through another frame containing wires, which divides it into tablets; these may be received upon racks and are ready for drying and stamping. It is needless to say that the slabs and tablets are cut with a view to reducing the amount of waste to the lowest possible limit. Such a machine, made by E. Forshaw & Son, Ltd., is shown in Fig. 14.

Fig. 12.—Barring machine.

Fig. 13.—Bar-cutting machine.

Fig. 14.—Tablet-cutting machine.

Open- and Close-piling.—As remarked previously, tallow soaps should be cut whilst warm, and the bars "open-piled," or stacked across each other in such a way that air has free access to each bar for a day. The bar of soap will skin or case-harden, and next day may be "close-piled," or placed in the storage bins, where they should remain for two or three weeks, when they will be in perfect condition for packing into boxes ready for distribution.

Fig. 15.—Soap stamp.

Drying.—"Oil soaps," as soaps of the washer type are termed, do not skin sufficiently by the open-piling treatment, and are generally exposed on racks to a current of hot air in a drying chamber in order to produce the skin, which prevents evaporation of water, and allows of an impression being given by the stamp without the soap adhering to the dies. It is of course understood that heavily liquored soaps are, as a rule, unsuitable for the drying treatment, as the bars become unshapely, and lose water rapidly.

Stamping.—Bar soaps are usually stamped by means of a hand-stamp containing removable or fixed brass letters (Fig. 15), with a certain brand or designation of quality and the name of the manufacturer or vendor, and are now ready for packing into boxes.

A very large bulk of the soap trade consists of the household quality in tablet form, readily divided into two cakes. These are stamped in the ordinary box moulds with two dies—top and bottom impressions—the die-plates, being removable, allow the impressions to be changed. This type of mould (Fig. 16) can be adjusted for the compression of tablets of varying thickness, the box preventing the escape of soap. We are indebted to E. Forshaw & Son, Ltd., for this illustration.

Fig. 16.—Box mould.

The stamping machine may be worked by hand (Fig. 17) or power driven. Where large quantities of a particular tablet have to be stamped, one of the many automatic mechanical stampers in existence may be employed, the tablets being conveyed to and from the dies by means of endless belts. Such a machine is shown in the accompanying illustration (Fig. 18).

If necessary, the soap is transferred to racks and exposed to the air, after which it is ready for wrapping, which is generally performed by manual labour, although in some instances automatic wrapping machines are in use.

Cardboard cartons are also used for encasing the wrapped tablets, the object being that these are more conveniently handled by tradesmen and may be advantageously used to form an attractive window display.

Cooling.—Many attempts have been made to shorten the time required for the framing and finishing of soap, by cooling the liquid soap as it leaves the pan.

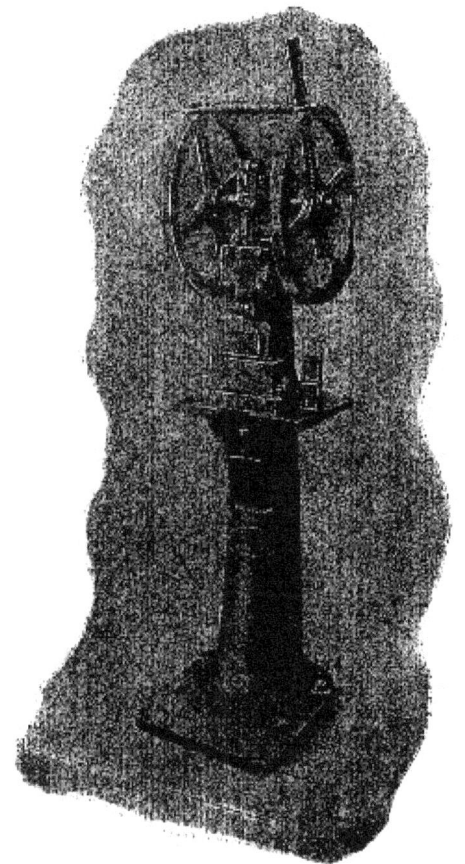

Fig. 17.—Soap-stamping machine, showing box mould.

With milling base, this is successfully accomplished in the Cressonnières' plant, by allowing the hot soap to fall upon the periphery of a revolving drum which can be cooled internally by means of water.

Fig. 18.—Automatic stamper.

In the case of household soaps, where the resultant product must be of good appearance and have a firm texture, the difficulty is to produce a bar fit for sale after the cooling has been performed, as soap which has been suddenly chilled lacks the appearance of that treated in the ordinary way. Several patents have been granted for various methods of moulding into bars in tubes, where the hot soap is cooled by being either surrounded by running water in a machine of similar construction to a candle machine, or rotated through a cooling medium; and numerous claims have been made both for mechanical appliances and for methods of removing or discharging the bars after cooling. In many instances these have proved unsatisfactory, owing to fracture of the crystalline structure. Moreover, in passing through some of the devices for solidification after chilling, the soap is churned by means of a worm or screw, and this interferes with the firmness of the finished bar, for, as is well known, soap which has been handled too much, does not regain its former firmness, and its appearance is rendered unsatisfactory.

A form of apparatus which is now giving satisfactory results is the Leimdoerfer continuous cooler (Fig. 19). This consists of a fixed charging hopper, A, a portable tank, B, containing tubes, and a detachable box, C, which can be raised or lowered by means of a screw, D. The bottom of the hopper is fitted with holes corresponding with the cooling tubes, e, and closed by plugs c, attached to a frame b, which terminates above in a screw spindle a, by means of which the frame and plugs can be raised and lowered so as to permit or stop the outflow of soap into the cooling tubes. The tubes are closed at the bottom by slides d, and the box B, in which they are mounted, is carried on a truck running on rails. The charging hopper can be connected with the soap-pan by a pipe, and when the hopper is filled with liquid soap the plugs c are raised and the air in the box C exhausted, thus causing the soap to descend into the cooling tubes.

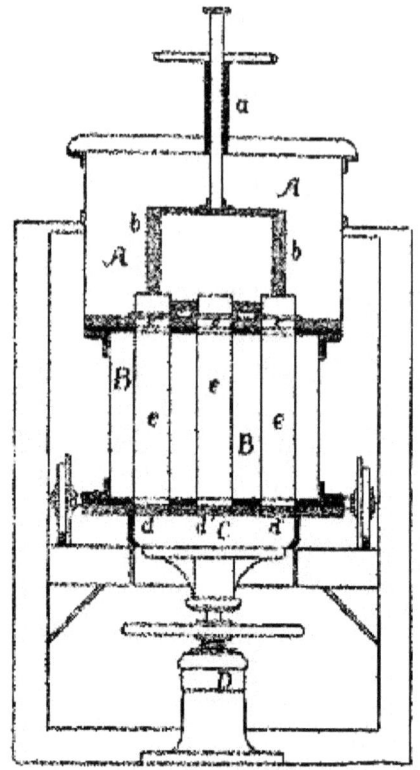

Fig. 19.—Leimdoerfer cooler.

The slides *d* are closed, the screw D released, and the box B moved away to make room for another. At the end of the rail track is an ejecting device which pushes the cooled soap out of the tubes, and the truck is run back on a side track to the machine for use over again. In this way the apparatus can be worked continuously, the soap being received from the cooling pipes on a suitable arrangement for transport to the press or store room.

A similar idea has been made the subject of a patent by Holoubek (Eng. Pat. 24,440, 1904, Fig. 20). The soap is run into frames or moulds having open sides, which are closed by being clamped with screws and pressure plates between cooling tubes through which water circulates.

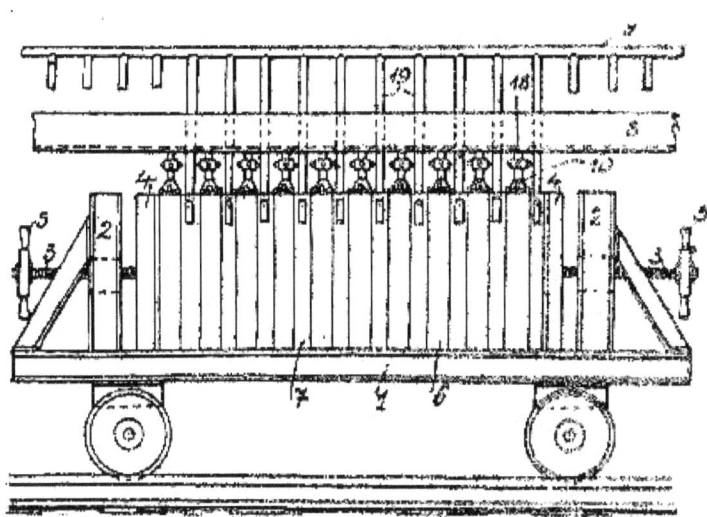

Fig. 20.—Holoubek's cooler.

CHAPTER VII.

TOILET, TEXTILE AND MISCELLANEOUS SOAPS.

Toilet Soaps—Cold Process Soaps—Settled Boiled Soaps—Remelted Soaps—Milled Soaps—Drying—Milling and Incorporating Colour, Perfume, or Medicament—Perfume—Colouring Matter—Neutralising and Superfatting Material—Compressing—Cutting—Stamping—Medicated Soaps—Ether Soap—Floating Soaps—Shaving Soaps—Textile Soaps—Soaps for Woollen, Cotton and Silk Industries—Patent Textile Soaps—Miscellaneous Soaps.

Toilet Soaps.—By the term "toilet soap" is inferred a soap specially adapted for toilet use by reason not only of its good detergent and lathering qualities, but also on account of its freedom from caustic alkali and any other ingredient likely to cause irritation or injury to the skin.

Toilet soaps may be simply classified according to their method of preparation into the following four classes:—

(1) Cold process soaps.
(2) Settled boiled soaps.
(3) Remelted soaps.
(4) Milled soaps.

Soaps of the first class are of comparatively trifling importance, having been superseded by the other qualities. Details of the "cold process" have already been given on page 46; it is only necessary to add the desired perfume and colouring matter to the soap.

The second class consists of good quality settled soaps, direct from the copper, to which have been added, prior to framing, suitable perfume and colouring matter, also, if necessary, dealkalising materials.

The third class is represented by soaps made by the old English method of remelting, which are often termed "perfumers'," or "little pan" soaps. The soap-base or mixture of various kinds of soap is remelted in a steam-jacketed pan, or pan provided with steam coils, and agitated. The agitation must not be too vigorous or lengthy, or the soap will become aerated. When all the soap is molten, additions of pearl ash solution are made to give it a finer and smoother texture, render it more transparent, and increase its lathering properties. The necessary colour, in a soluble form, is well incorporated, and lastly the perfume. Owing to volatilisation, much of the perfume is lost when added to hot soap, and it is necessary to add a large quantity to get the desired odour; hence the cheaper essential oils have to be used, so that the perfume of this class of soap is not so delicate as that of milled soaps, although it is quite possible to produce remelted soaps as free from uncombined alkali as a milled toilet soap.

Palm-oil soap often forms the basis for yellow and brown toilet soaps of this class. The old-fashioned Brown Windsor soap was originally a curd soap that with age and frequent remelting had acquired a brown tint by oxidation of the fatty acids—the oftener remelted the better the resultant soap.

Medicaments are sometimes added to these soaps, *e.g.*, camphor, borax, coal-tar, or carbolic. Oatmeal and bran have been recommended in combination with soap for toilet purposes, and a patent (Eng. Pat. 26,396, 1896) has been granted for the use of these substances together with wood-fibre impregnated with boric acid.

After cooling in small frames, the soap is slabbed, and cut into blocks, and finally into portions suitable for stamping in a press (hand or steam driven) with a design or lettering on each side.

Milled Toilet Soaps.—Practically all high-class soaps now on the market pass through the French or milling process. This treatment, as its name implies, was first practised by the French who introduced it to this country, and consists briefly of (i.) drying, (ii.) milling and incorporating colour, perfume or medicament, (iii.) compressing, and (iv.) cutting and stamping.

The advantages of milled soap over toilet soap produced by other methods are that the former, containing less water and more actual soap, is more economical in use, possesses a better appearance, and more elegant finish, does not shrink or lose its shape, is more uniform in composition, and essential oils and delicate perfumes may be incorporated without fear of loss or deterioration.

Only soap made from best quality fats is usually milled, a suitable base being that obtained by saponifying a blend of the finest white tallow with a proportion, not exceeding 25 per cent., of cocoa-nut oil, and prepared as described in Chapter V.

The first essential of a milling base is that the saponification should be thorough and complete; if this is not ensured, rancidity is liable to occur and a satisfactory toilet soap cannot be produced. The soap must not be short in texture or brittle and liable to split, but of a firm and somewhat plastic consistency.

(i.) *Drying.*—The milling-base, after solidification in the frames, contains almost invariably from 28 to 30 per cent. of water, and this quantity must be reduced to rather less than half before the soap can be satisfactorily milled.

Cutting the soap into bars or strips and open piling greatly facilitates the drying, which is usually effected by chipping the soap and exposing it on trays to a current of hot air at 95-105° F. (35-40° C.).

There are several forms of drying chambers in which the trays of chips are placed upon a series of racks one above another, and warm air circulated through, and Fig. 21 shows a soap drying apparatus with fan made by W. J. Fraser & Co., Ltd., London.

The older method of heating the air by allowing it to pass over a pipe or flue through which the products of combustion from a coke or coal fire are proceeding under the floor of the drying chamber to a small shaft, has been superseded by steam heat. The air is either drawn or forced by means of quickly revolving fans through a cylinder placed in a horizontal position and containing steam coils, or passed over steam-pipes laid under the iron grating forming the floor of the chamber.

Fig. 21.—Soap-drying apparatus.

It will be readily understood that in the case of a bad conductor of heat, like soap-chippings, it is difficult to evaporate moisture without constantly moving them and exposing fresh surfaces to the action of heat.

In the Cressonnières' system, where the shavings of chilled soap are dried by being carried through a heated chamber upon a series of endless bands (the first discharging the contents on to a lower belt which projects at the end, and is moving in the opposite direction, and so on), this is performed by intercepting milling rollers in the system of belts (Eng. Pat. 4,916, 1898) whereby the surfaces exposed to the drying are altered, and it is claimed that the formation of hardened crust is prevented.

In the ordinary methods of drying, the chips are frequently moved by hand to assist uniform evaporation.

The degree of saturation of the air with moisture must be taken into consideration in regulating the temperature and flow of air through the drying chamber, and for this purpose the use of a hygrometer is advantageous.

It is very important that the correct amount of moisture should be left in the soap, not too much, nor too little; the exact point can only be determined by judgment and experience, and depends to a considerable extent upon the nature of the soap, and also on the amount of perfume or medicament to be added, but speaking generally, a range of 11 to 14 per cent. gives good results. If the soap contains less than this amount it is liable to crumble during the milling, will not compress satisfactorily, and the finished tablet may have a tendency to crack and contain gritty particles so objectionable in use. If, on the other hand, the soap is left too moist, it is apt to stick to the rollers and mill with difficulty, and during compression the surface assumes a blistered and sticky appearance.

(ii.) *Milling and Incorporation of Colour, Perfume or Medicament.*—The object of milling is to render the soap perfectly homogeneous, and to reduce it to a state in which colour, perfume, or any necessary neutralising material or other substance may be thoroughly incorporated. The milling machine consists of smooth granite rollers, fitted with suitable gearing and working in an iron framework (Fig. 22). The rollers are connected in such a manner that they rotate at different speeds, and this increases the efficiency of the milling, and ensures that the action of the rollers is one of rubbing rather than crushing.

By means of suitably arranged screws the pressure of the rollers on one another can be adjusted to give the issuing soap any desired thickness; care should be taken that the sheets of soap are not unnecessarily thick or the colour and odour will not be uniform.

The soap, in the form of chips, is introduced on to the rollers through a hopper, and after one passage through the mill, from bottom to top, one of the serrated knife edges is applied and the ribbons of the soap are delivered into the top of the hopper where the colour, perfume, and any other desired admixture is added, and the milling operation repeated three or four times. When the incorporation is complete the other scraper is fixed against the top roller and the soap ribbon passed into the receptacle from which it is conveyed to the compressor. A better plan, however, especially in the case of the best grade soaps, where the perfumes added are necessarily more delicate and costly, is to make the addition of the perfume when the colour has been thoroughly mixed throughout the mass. Another method is to mill once and transfer the mass to a rotary mixing machine, fitted with internal blades, of a peculiar form, which revolve in opposite directions one within the other as the mixer is rotated. The perfume, colouring matter, etc., are added and the mixer closed and set in motion, when, after a short time, the soap is reduced to a fine granular condition, with the colour and perfume evenly distributed throughout the whole. By the use of such machines, the loss of perfume by evaporation, which during milling is quite appreciable, is reduced to a minimum, and the delicacy of the aroma is preserved unimpaired.

Fig. 22.—Milling machine.

Prolonged milling, especially with a suitable soap base, tends to produce a semi-transparent appearance, which is admired by some, but the increased cost of production by the repeated milling is not accompanied by any real improvement in the soap.

Perfume.—The materials used in perfuming soap will be dealt with fully in the next chapter. The quantity necessary to be added varies considerably with the nature of the essential oils, and also the price at which the soap is intended to be sold. In the cheaper grades of milled soaps the quantity will range from 10-30 fluid ozs. per cwt., and but rarely exceeds 18-20 ozs., whereas in more costly soaps as much as 40-50 fluid ozs. are sometimes added to the cwt.

Colouring Matter.—During recent years an outcry has been made against highly coloured soaps, and the highest class soaps have been manufactured either colourless or at the most with only a very delicate tint. It is obvious that a white soap guarantees the use of only the highest grade oils and fats, and excludes the introduction of any rosin, and, so far, the desire for a white soap is doubtless justified. Many perfumes, however, tend to quickly discolour a soap, hence the advantage of giving it a slight tint. For this purpose a vegetable colouring matter is preferable, and chlorophyll is very suitable.

Fig. 23.—Compressor.

A demand still exists for brightly coloured soaps, and this is usually met by the use of coal-tar dyes. The quantity required is of course extremely small, so that no harm or disagreeable result could possibly arise from their use.

Neutralising and Superfatting Material.—If desired, the final neutralisation of free alkali can be carried out during the milling process, any superfatting material being added at the same time. The chief neutralising reagents have already been mentioned in Chapter VI.

With regard to superfatting material, the quantity of this should be very small, not exceeding 6-8 ozs. per cwt: The most suitable materials are vaseline, lanoline, or spermaceti.

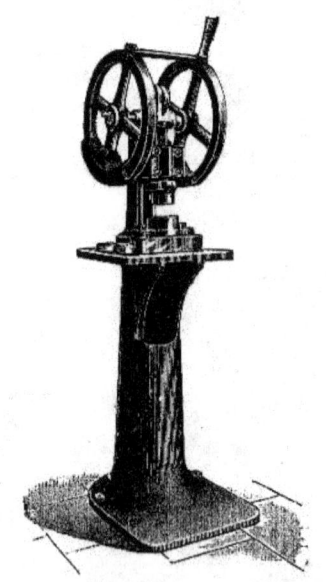

Fig. 24—Hand soap-stamping press.

(iii.) *Compressing.*—The next stage is the compression and binding of the soap ribbons into a solid bar suitable for stamping, and the plant used (Fig. 23) for this purpose is substantially the same in all factories. The soap is fed through a hopper into a strong metal conical-shaped tube like a cannon, which tapers towards the nozzle, and in which a single or twin screw is moving, and the soap is thereby forced through a perforated metallic disc, subjected to great pressure, and compressed. The screws must be kept uniformly covered with shavings during compression to obviate air bubbles in the soap.

Fig. 25.—Screw press.

The soap finally emerges through the nozzle (to which is attached a cutter of suitable shape and size according to the form it is intended the final tablet to take) as a long, polished, solid bar, which is cut with a knife or wire into lengths of 2 or 3 feet, and if of satisfactory appearance, is ready for cutting and stamping. The nozzle of the plodder is heated by means of a Bunsen burner to about 120° or 130°

F. (49°-55° C.) to allow the soap to be easily forced out, and this also imparts a good gloss and finish to the ejected bar—if the nozzle is too hot, however, the soap will be blistered, whereas insufficient heat will result in streaky soap of a poor and dull appearance.

(iv.) *Cutting and Stamping.*—In cutting the soap into sections for stamping, the cutter should shape it somewhat similar to the required finished tablet.

Many manufacturers cut the soap into sections having concave ends, and in stamping, the corners are forced into the concavity, with the result that unsightly markings are produced at each end of the tablet. It is preferable to have a cutter with convex ends, and if the stamping is to be done in a pin mould the shape should be a trifle larger than the exact size of the desired tablet.

Fig. 26—Pin mould.

The stamping may be performed by a hand stamper (Fig. 24), a screw press (Fig. 25), or by a steam stamper. The screw press works very satisfactorily for toilet soaps.

There are two kinds of moulds in use for milled soaps:—

(*a*) *Pin Moulds* in which tablets of one size and shape only can be produced (Fig. 25). The edges of the mould meet very exactly, the upper part of the die carries two pins attached to the shoulder, and these are received into two holes in the shoulder of the bottom plate. The superfluous soap is forced out as the dies meet.

(*b*) *Band or Collar Moulds.*—In this form (Fig, 27) the mould may be adjusted to stamp various sized tablets, say from 2 ozs. to 5-1/3 ozs. and different impressions given by means of removable die plates. The band or collar prevents the soap squeezing out sideways. We are indebted to R. Forehaw & Son, Ltd., for the loan of this illustration.

It is usual to moisten the soap or mould with a dilute solution of glycerine if it should have a tendency to stick to the die plates.

The soap is then ready for final trimming, wrapping, and boxing.

Fig. 27—Band Mould.

Medicated Soaps.

The inherent cleansing power of soap renders it invaluable in combating disease, while it also has distinct germicidal properties, a 2 per cent. solution proving fatal to B. coli communis in less than six hours, and even a 1 per cent. solution having a marked action on germs in fifteen minutes.

Many makers, however, seek more or less successfully to still further increase the value of soap in this direction by the incorporation of various drugs and chemicals; and the number of medicated soaps on the market is now very large. Such soaps may consist of either hard or soft soaps to which certain medicaments have been added, and can be roughly divided into two classes, (*a*) those which contain a specific for various definite diseases, the intention being that the remedy should be absorbed by the pores of the skin and thus penetrate the system, and (*b*) those impregnated with chemicals intended to act as antiseptics or germicides, or, generally, as disinfectants.

The preparation of medicinal soaps appears to have been first taken up in a scientific manner by Unna of Hamburg in 1886, who advocated the use of soap in preference to plasters as a vehicle for the application of certain remedies.

Theoretically, he considered a soap-stock made entirely from beef tallow the most suitable for the purpose, but in practice found that the best results were obtained by using a superfatted soap made from a blend of one part of olive oil with eight parts of beef tallow, saponified with a mixture of two parts of soda to one part of potash, sufficient fat being employed to leave an excess of 3 or 4 per cent. unsaponified. Recent researches have shown, however, that even if a superfatted soap-base is beneficial for the preparation of toilet soaps (a point which is open to doubt), it is quite inadmissible for the manufacture of germicidal and disinfectant soaps, the bactericidal efficiency of which is much restricted by the presence of free fat.

Many of the medicaments added to soaps require special methods of incorporation therein, as they otherwise react with the soap and decompose it, forming comparatively inert compounds. This applies particularly to salts of mercury, such as *corrosive sublimate* or mercuric chloride, and *biniodide of mercury*, both of which have very considerable germicidal power, and are consequently frequently added to soaps. If simply mixed with the soap in the mill, reaction very quickly takes place between the mercury salt and the soap, with formation of the insoluble mercury compounds of the fatty acids, a change which can be readily seen to occur in such a soap by the rapid development on keeping, of a dull slaty-green appearance. Numerous processes have been suggested, and in some cases patented, to overcome this difficulty. In the case of corrosive sublimate, Geissler suggested that the soap to which this reagent is to be added should contain an excess of fatty acids, and would thereby be rendered stable. This salt has also been incorporated with milled soap in a dry state in conjunction with ammonio-mercuric chloride, β-naphthol, methyl salicylate, and eucalyptol. It is claimed that these bodies are present in an unchanged condition, and become active when the soap is added to water as in washing. Ehrhardt (Eng. Pat. 2,407, 1898) patented a method of making antiseptic mercury soap by using mercury albuminate—a combination of mercuric chloride and casein, which is soluble in alkali, and added to the soap in an alkaline solution.

With biniodide of mercury the interaction can be readily obviated by adding to the biniodide of mercury an equal weight of potassium iodide. This process, devised and patented by J. Thomson in 1886, has been worked since that time with extremely satisfactory results. Strengths of 1/2, 1, and 3 per cent. biniodide are sold, but owing to the readiness with which it is absorbed by the skin a soap containing more than 1/2 per cent. should only be used under medical advice.

A similar combination of *bromide of mercury* with potassium, sodium, or ammonium bromide has recently been patented by Cooke for admixture with liquid, hard, or soft soaps.

Zinc and other Metallic Salts.—At various times salts of metals other than mercury have been added to soap, but, owing to their insolubility in water, their efficiency as medicaments is very trifling or nil. Compounds have been formed of metallic oxides and other salts with oleic said, and mixtures made with vaseline and lanoline, and incorporated with soap, but they have not met with much success.

Another chemical commonly added to soap is *Borax*. In view of its alkaline reaction to litmus, turning red litmus blue, this salt is no doubt generally regarded as alkaline, and, as such, without action on soap. On the contrary, however, it is an acid salt containing an excess of boric acid over the soda present, hence when it is added to soap, fatty acids are necessarily liberated, causing the soap to quickly become rancid. As a remedy for this it has been proposed to add sufficient alkali to convert the borax into neutral monoborate of soda which is then added to the soap. This process is patented and the name "Kastilis" has been given to the neutral salt. The incorporation of borax with the addition of gum tragasol forms the subject of two patents (Eng. Pats. 4,415, 1904; and 25,425, 1905); increased detergent and lasting properties are claimed for the soap. Another patented process (Eng. Pat. 17,218, 1904) consists of coating the borax with a protective layer of fat or wax before adding to the soap with the idea that reaction will not take place until required. *Boric acid* possesses the defects of borax in a greater degree, and would, of course, simply form sodium borate with liberation of fatty acids, so should never be added to a neutral soap.

Salicylic Acid is often recommended for certain skin diseases, and here again the addition of the acid to soap under ordinary conditions results in the formation of sodium salicylate and free fatty acids.

To overcome this a process has recently been patented for rubbing the acid up with vaseline before addition to soap, but the simplest way appears to be to add the soda salt of the acid to soap.

Amongst the more common milled medicated toilet soaps may be mentioned, in addition to the above:—

Birch Tar Soap, containing 5 or 10 per cent. birch tar, which has a characteristic pungent odour and is recommended as a remedy for eczema and psoriasis.

Carbolic Soap.—A toilet soap should not contain more than 3 per cent. of pure phenol, for with larger quantities irritation is likely to be experienced by susceptible skins.

Coal Tar.—These soaps contain, in addition to carbolic acid and its homologues, naphthalene and other hydrocarbons derived from coal, naphthol, bases, etc. Various blends of different fractions of coal tar are used, but the most valuable constituents from a disinfectant point of view are undoubtedly the phenols, or tar acids, though in this case as with carbolic and cresylic soaps, the amount of phenols should not exceed 3 per cent. in a toilet soap. An excess of naphthalene should also be avoided, since, on account of its strong odour, soaps containing much of it are unpopular. The odour of coal tar is considerably modified by and blends well with a perfume containing oils of cassia, lavender, spike, and red thyme.

Formaldehyde.—This substance is one of the most powerful disinfectants known, and it may be readily introduced into soap without undergoing any decomposition, by milling in 2-3 per cent. of formalin, a 40 per cent. aqueous solution of formaldehyde, which is a gas. White soaps containing this chemical retain their whiteness almost indefinitely.

New combinations of formaldehyde with other bodies are constantly being brought forward as disinfectants. Among others the compound resulting from heating lanoline with formaldehyde has been patented (Eng. Pat. 7,169, 1898), and is recommended as an antiseptic medicament for incorporation with soap.

Glycerine.—Nearly all soaps contain a small quantity of this body which is not separated in the lyes. In some cases, however, a much larger quantity is desired, up to some 6 or 8 per cent. To mill this in requires great care, otherwise the soap tends to blister during compression. The best way is to dry the soap somewhat further than usual, till it contains say only 9 or 10 per cent. moisture and then mill in the glycerine.

Ichthyol or *Ammonium-Ichthyol-Sulphonate* is prepared by treating with sulphuric acid, and afterwards with ammonia, the hydrocarbon oil containing sulphur obtained by the dry distillation of the fossil remains of fish and sea-animals, which form a bituminous mineral deposit in Germany. This product has been admixed with soap for many years, the quantity generally used being about 5 per cent.; the resultant soap is possessed of a characteristic empyreumatic smell, very dark colour, and is recommended for rosacea and various skin diseases, and also as an anti-rheumatic.

Ichthyol has somewhat changed its character during recent years, being now almost completely soluble in water, and stronger in odour than formerly.

Iodine.—A soap containing iodine is sometimes used in scrofulous skin diseases. It should contain some 3 per cent. iodine, while potassium iodide should also be added to render the iodine soluble.

Lysol.—This name is applied to a soap solution of cresol, "Lysol Soap" being simply another form of coal-tar soap. The usual strength is 10 per cent. lysol, and constitutes a patented article (Fr. Pat. 359,061, 1905).

Naphthol.—β-Naphthol, also a coal-tar derivative, is a good germicide, and, incorporated in soap to the extent of 3 per cent. together with sulphur, is recommended for scabies, eczema and many other cutaneous affections.

Sulphur.—Since sulphur is insoluble in water, its action when used in conjunction with soap can be but very slow and slight. Sulphur soaps are, however, very commonly sold, and 10 per cent. is the strength usually advocated, though many so-called sulphur soaps actually contain very little sulphur. They are said to be efficacious for acne and rosacea.

Sulphur soaps, when dissolved in water, gradually generate sulphuretted hydrogen, which, although characteristic, makes their use disagreeable and lessens their popular estimation.

Terebene.—The addition of this substance to soap, though imparting a very refreshing and pleasant odour, does not materially increase the disinfectant value of the soap. A suitable strength is 5 per cent.

Thymol.—This furnishes a not unpleasant, and very useful antiseptic soap, recommended especially for the cleansing of ulcerated wounds and restoring the skin to a healthy state. The normal strength is 3 per cent. It is preferable to replace part of the thymol with red thyme oil, the thymene of which imparts a sweeter odour to the soap than if produced with thymol alone. A suitable blend is 2-1/2 per cent. of thymol crystals and 1-1/2 per cent. of a good red thyme oil.

Of the vast number of less known proposed additions to toilet soaps, mention may be made in passing of:—

Fluorides.—These have been somewhat popular during recent years for the disinfection of breweries, etc., and also used to some extent as food preservatives. Of course only neutral fluorides are available for use in soap, acid fluorides and soap being obviously incompatible. In the authors' experience, however, sodium fluoride appears to have little value as a germicide when added to soap, such soaps being found to rapidly become rancid and change colour.

Albumen.—The use of albumen—egg, milk, and vegetable—in soap has been persistently advocated in this country during the past few years. The claims attributed to albumen are, that it neutralises free alkali, causes the soap to yield a more copious lather, and helps to bind it more closely, and a further inducement held out is that it allows more water to be left in the soap without affecting its firmness. Experiments made by the authors did not appear to justify any enthusiasm on the subject, and the use of albumen for soap-making in this country appears to be very slight, however popular it may be on the Continent. Numerous other substances have been proposed for addition to soaps, including yeast, tar from peat (sphagnol), Swedish wood tar, permanganate of potash, perborates and percarbonates of soda and ammonia, chlorine compounds, but none of these has at present come much into favour, and some had only ephemeral existence. Of the many drugs that it has been suggested to admix in soap for use in allaying an irritable condition of the skin, the majority are obviously better applied in the form of ointments, and we need not consider them further.

Ether Soap.—Another form of medicated soap made by a few firms is a liquid ether soap containing mercuric iodide, and intended for surgeons' use. This, as a rule, consists of a soap made from olive oil and potash, dissolved in alcohol and mixed with ether, the mercuric iodide being dissolved in a few drops of water containing an equal weight of potassium iodide, and this solution added to the alcohol-ether soap.

Floating Soaps.—Attempts have been made to produce tablets of soap that will float upon the surface of water, by inserting cork, or floats, or a metallic plate in such a manner that there is an air space between the metal and the soap. The more usual method is to incorporate into hot soap sufficient air, by means of a specially designed self-contained jacketed crutcher, in which two shafts carrying small blades or paddles rotate in opposite directions, to reduce the density of the soap below that of water and so enable the compressed tablet to float. The difference in weight of a tablet of the same size before and after aerating amounts to 10 per cent.

Ordinary milling soap is used as a basis for this soap; the settled soap direct from the copper at 170° F. (77° C.) is carefully neutralised with bicarbonate of sodium, oleic or stearic acids, or boro-glyceride, perfumed and aerated.

Floating soap, which is usually white (some are of a cream tint), cannot be recommended as economical, whilst its deficiency in lathering properties, owing to occluded air, is a serious drawback to its popularity as a toilet detergent.

Shaving Soaps.—The first essential of a shaving soap, apart from its freedom from caustic alkali or any substance exerting an irritating effect upon the skin, is the quick production of a profuse creamy lather which is lasting. Gum tragacanth is used in some cases to give lasting power or durability, but is not necessary, as this property is readily attained by the use of a suitable proportion of potash soap. The best shaving soaps are mixtures of various proportions of neutral soda and potash soaps, produced by the combination of ordinary milling base with a white potash soap, either melted or milled together. Glycerine is sometimes added, and is more satisfactorily milled in.

Every precaution should be taken to ensure thorough saponification of the soaps intended for blending in shaving soap, otherwise there will be a tendency to become discoloured and develop rancidity with age. Shaving soaps are delicately perfumed, and are placed on the market either in the form of sticks which are cut from the bar of soap as it leaves the compressor, or stamped in flat cakes.

Shaving creams and pastes are of the same nature as shaving soaps, but usually contain a larger proportion of superfatting material and considerably more water.

TEXTILE SOAPS.

In the woollen, cloth, and silk textile industries, the use of soap for detergent and emulsifying purposes is necessary in several of the processes, and the following is a brief description of the kinds of soap successfully employed in the various stages.

1. *Woollen Industry.*—The scouring of wool is the most important operation—it is the first treatment raw wool is subjected to, and if it is not performed in an efficient manner, gives rise to serious subsequent troubles to manufacturer, dyer, and finisher.

The object of scouring wool is to remove the wool-fat and wool perspiration (exuded from the skin of sheep), consisting of cholesterol and isocholesterol, and potassium salts of fatty acids, together with other salts, such as sulphates, chlorides, and phosphates. This is effected by washing in a warm dilute soap solution, containing in the case of low quality wool, a little carbonate of soda; the fatty matter is thereby emulsified and easily removed.

Soap, to be suitable for the purpose, must be free from uncombined caustic alkali, unsaponified fat, silicates, and rosin.

Wool can be dissolved in a moderately dilute solution of caustic soda, and the presence of this latter in soap, even in small quantities, is therefore liable to injure the fibres and make the resultant fabric possess a harsh "feel," and be devoid of lustre.

Unsaponified fat denotes badly made soap—besides reducing the emulsifying power of the liberated alkali, this fat may be absorbed by the fibres and not only induce rancidity but also cause trouble in dyeing.

Soaps containing silicates may have a deleterious action upon the fibres, causing them to become damaged and broken.

By general consent soaps containing rosin are unsuitable for use by woollen manufacturers, as they produce sticky insoluble lime and magnesia compounds which are deposited upon the fibres, and give rise to unevenness in the dyeing.

A neutral olive-oil soft soap is undoubtedly the best for the purpose of wool scouring, as, owing to its ready solubility in water, it quickly penetrates the fibres, is easily washed out, and produces a good "feel" so essential in the best goods, and tends to preserve the lustre and pliability of the fibre.

The high price of olive-oil soap, however, renders its use prohibitive for lower class goods, and in such cases no better soap can be suggested than the old-fashioned curd mottled or curd soaps (boiled very dry), as free as possible from uncombined caustic alkali. The raw wool, after this cleansing operation, is oiled with olive oil or oleine, prior to spinning; after spinning and weaving, the fabric, in the form of yarn or cloth, has to be scoured to free it from oil. The soap in most general use for scouring woollen fabrics is neutral oleine-soda soap. Some manufacturers prefer a cheap curd soap, such as is generally termed "second curd," and in cases where lower grades of wools are handled, the user is often willing to have soap containing rosin (owing to its cheapness) and considers a little alkalinity desirable to assist in removing the oil.

Another operation in which soap is used, is that of milling or fulling, whereby the fabric is made to shrink and thus becomes more compact and closer in texture. The fabric is thoroughly cleansed, for which purpose the soap should be neutral and free from rosin and silicates, otherwise a harsh feeling or stickiness will be produced. Curd soaps or finely-fitted soaps made from tallow or bleached palm oil, with or without the addition of cocoa-nut oil, give the best results. All traces of soap must be carefully removed if the fabric is to be dyed.

The woollen dyer uses soap on the dyed pieces to assist the milling, and finds that a good soap, made from either olive oil, bleached palm oil, or tallow, is preferable, and, although it is generally specified to be free from alkali, a little alkalinity is not of consequence, for the woollen goods are, as a rule, acid after dyeing, and this alkalinity would be instantly neutralised.

2. *Cotton Industry.*—Cotton fibres are unacted upon by caustic alkali, so that the soap used in cleaning and preparing cotton goods for dyeing need not be neutral, in fact alkalinity is a distinct advantage in order to assist the cleansing.

Any curd soap made from tallow, with or without the addition of a small quantity of cocoa-nut oil, may be advantageously used for removing the natural oil.

In cotton dyeing, additions of soap are often made to the bath, and in such cases the soap must be of good odour and neutral, lest the colours should be acted upon and tints altered. Soaps made from olive oil and palm oil are recommended. The same kind of soap is sometimes used for soaping the dyed cotton goods.

The calico-printer uses considerable quantities of soap for cleansing the printed-cloths. The soap not only cleanses by helping to remove the gummy and starchy constituents of the adhering printing paste, but also plays an important part in fixing and brightening the colours. Soaps intended for this class of work must be quite neutral (to obviate any possible alteration in colour by the action of free alkali), free from objectionable odour and rosin, and readily soluble in water. These qualities are possessed by olive-oil soaps, either soft or hard. A neutral olive-oil soft soap, owing to its solubility in cold water, may be used for fibres coloured with most delicate dyes, which would be fugitive in hot soap solutions, and this soap is employed for the most expensive work.

Olive-oil curd (soda) soaps are in general use; those made from palm oil are also recommended, although they are not so soluble as the olive-oil soaps. Tallow curd soaps are sometimes used, but the difficulty with which they dissolve is a drawback, and renders them somewhat unsuitable.

3. *Silk Industry.*—Silk is secured to remove the sericin or silk-glue and adhering matter from the raw silk, producing thereby lustre on the softened fibre and thus preparing it for the dyer.

The very best soap for the purpose is an olive-oil soft soap; olive-oil and oleine hard soaps may also be used. The soap is often used in conjunction with carbonate of soda to assist the removal of the sericin, but, whilst carbonates are permissible, it is necessary to avoid an excess of caustic soda.

Tallow soaps are so slowly soluble that they are not applicable to the scouring of silk.

The dyer of silk requires soap, which is neutral and of a pleasant odour. The preference is given to neutral olive-oil soft soap, but hard soaps (made from olive oil, oleine, or palm oil) are used chiefly on account of cheapness. It is essential, however, that the soap should be free from rosin on account of its frequent use and consequent decomposition in the acid dye bath, when any liberated rosin acids would cling to the silk fibres and produce disagreeable results.

Patent Textile Soaps.—Stockhausen (Eng. Pat. 24,868, 1897) makes special claim for a soap, termed Monopole Soap, to be used in place of Turkey-red oils in the dyeing and printing of cotton goods and finishing of textile fabrics.

The soap is prepared by heating the sulphonated oil (obtained on treatment of castor oil with sulphuric acid) with alkali, and it is stated that the product is not precipitated when used in the dye-bath as is ordinary soap, nor is it deposited upon the fibres.

Another patent (Eng. Pat. 16,382, 1897), has for its object the obviating of the injurious effects upon wool, of alkali liberated from a solution of soap. It is proposed to accomplish this by sulphonating part of the fat used in making the soap.

Miscellaneous Soaps.—Under this heading may be classed soaps intended for special purposes and consisting essentially of ordinary boiled soap to which additions of various substances have been made.

With additions of naphtha, fractions of petroleum, and turpentine, the detergent power of the soap is increased by the action of these substances in removing grease.

Amongst the many other additions may be mentioned: ox-gall or derivatives therefrom (for carpet-cleaning soap), alkali sulphides (for use of lead-workers), aniline colours (for home-dyeing soaps), pumice and tripoli (motorists' soaps), pine-needle oil, in some instances together with lanoline (for massage soaps), pearl-ash (for soap intended to remove oil and tar stains), magnesia, rouge, ammonium carbonate, chalk (silversmiths' soap), powdered orris, precipitated chalk, magnesium carbonate (tooth soaps).

Soap powders or dry soaps are powdered mixtures of soap, soda ash, or soda crystals, and other chemicals, whilst polishing soaps often contain from 85 to 90 per cent. siliceous matter, and can scarcely be termed soap.

CHAPTER VIII.

SOAP PERFUMES.

Essential Oils—Source and Preparation—Properties—Artificial and Synthetic Perfumes.

The number of raw materials, both natural and artificial, at the disposal of the perfumer, has increased so enormously during recent years that the scenting of soaps has now become an art requiring very considerable skill, and a thorough knowledge of the products to be handled. Not only does the all-important question of odour come into consideration, but the action of the perfumes on the soap, and on each other, has also to be taken into account. Thus, many essential oils and synthetic perfumes cause the soap to darken rapidly on keeping, *e.g.*, clove oil, cassia oil, heliotropin, vanillin. Further, some odoriferous substances, from their chemical nature, are incompatible with soap, and soon decompose any soap to which they are added, while in a few cases, the blending of two unsuitable perfumes results, by mutual reaction, in the effect of each being lost. In the case of oils like bergamot oil, the odour value of which depends chiefly on their ester content, it is very important that these should not be added to soaps containing much free alkali, as these esters are readily decomposed thereby. Some perfumes possess the property of helping the soap to retain other and more delicate odours considerably longer than would otherwise be possible. Such perfumes are known as "fixing agents" or "fixateurs," and among the most important of these may be mentioned musk, both natural and artificial, civet, the oils of Peru balsam, sandalwood, and patchouli, and benzyl benzoate.

The natural perfumes employed for addition to soaps are almost entirely of vegetable origin, and consist of essential oils, balsams, and resins, animal perfumes such as musk, civet, and ambergris being reserved principally for the preparation of "extraits".

As would be expected with products of such diverse character, the methods employed for the preparation of essential oils vary considerably. Broadly speaking, however, the processes may be divided into three classes— (1) *expression*, used for orange, lemon, and lime oils; (2) *distillation*, employed for otto of rose, geranium, sandalwood, and many other oils; and (3) *extraction*, including *enfleurage*, by which the volatile oil from the flowers is either first absorbed by a neutral fat such as lard, and then extracted therefrom by maceration in alcohol, or directly extracted from the flowers by means of a volatile solvent such as benzene, petroleum ether, or chloroform. The last process undoubtedly furnishes products most nearly resembling the natural floral odours, and is the only one which does not destroy the delicate fragrance of the violet and jasmine. The yield, however, is extremely small, and concrete perfumes prepared in this way are therefore somewhat costly.

The essential oils used are derived from upwards of twenty different botanical families, and are obtained from all parts of the world. Thus, from Africa we have geranium and clove oils; from America, bay, bois de rose, Canadian snake root, cedarwood, linaloe, peppermint, petitgrain, and sassafras; from Asia, camphor, cassia, cinnamon, patchouli, sandalwood, star anise, ylang-ylang, and the grass oils, *viz.*, citronella, lemongrass, palmarosa, and vetivert; from Australia, eucalyptus; while in Europe there are the citrus oils, bergamot, lemon, and orange, produced by Sicily, aspic, lavender, neroli, petitgrain, and rosemary by France, caraway and clove by Holland, anise by Russia, and otto of rose by Bulgaria.

Attempts have been made to classify essential oils either on a botanical basis or according to their chemical composition, but neither method is very satisfactory, and, in describing the chief constituents and properties of the more important oils, we have preferred therefore to arrange them alphabetically, as being simpler for reference.

It is a matter of some difficulty to judge the purity of essential oils, not only because of their complex nature, but owing to the very great effect upon their properties produced by growing the plants in different soils and under varying climatic conditions, and still more to the highly scientific methods of adulteration adopted by unscrupulous vendors. The following figures will be found, however, to include all normal oils.

Anise Stell, or *Star Anise*, from the fruit of Illicium verum, obtained from China. Specific gravity at 15° C., 0.980-0.990; optical rotation, faintly dextro- or lævo-rotatory, +0° 30' to -2°; refractive index at 20° C., 1.553-1.555; solidifying point, 14°-17° C.; solubility in 90 per cent. alcohol, 1 in 3 or 4.

The chief constituents of the oil are anethol, methyl chavicol, d-pinene, l-phellandrene, and in older oils, the oxidation products of anethol, *viz.* anisic aldehyde and anisic acid. Since anethol is the most valuable constituent, and the solidifying point of the oil is roughly proportional to its anethol content, oils with a higher solidifying point are the best.

Aspic oil, from the flowers of Lavandula spica, obtained from France and Spain, and extensively employed in perfuming household and cheap toilet soaps; also frequently found as an adulterant in lavender oil. Specific gravity at 15° C., 0.904-0.913; optical rotation, French, dextro-rotatory up to +4°, rarely up to +7°, Spanish, frequently slightly lævo-rotatory to -2°, or dextro-rotatory up to +7°; esters, calculated as linalyl acetate, 2 to 6 per cent.; most oils are soluble in 65 per cent. alcohol 1 in 4, in no case should more than 2.5 volumes of 70 per cent. alcohol be required for solution.

The chief constituents of the oil are: linalol, cineol, borneol, terpineol, geraniol, pinene, camphene and camphor.

Bay oil, distilled from the leaves of Pimenta acris, and obtained from St. Thomas and other West Indian Islands. It is used to some extent as a perfume for shaving soaps, but chiefly in the Bay Rhum toilet preparation. Specific gravity at 15° C., 0.965-0.980; optical rotation, slightly lævo-rotatory up to -3°; phenols, estimated by absorption with 5 per cent. caustic potash solution, from 45 to 60 per cent.; the oil is generally insoluble in 90 per cent. alcohol, though when freshly distilled it dissolves in its own volume of alcohol of this strength.

The oil contains eugenol, myrcene, chavicol, methyl eugenol, methyl chavicol, phellandrene, and citral.

Bergamot oil, obtained by expression from the fresh peel of the fruit of Citrus Bergamia, and used very largely for the perfuming of toilet soaps. Specific gravity at 15° C., 0.880-0.886; optical rotation, +10° to +20°; esters, calculated as linalyl acetate, 35-40 per cent., and occasionally as high as 42-43 per cent.; frequently soluble in 1.5 parts of 80 per cent. alcohol, or failing that, should dissolve in one volume of 82.5 or 85 per cent. alcohol. When evaporated on the water-bath the oil should not leave more than 5-6 per cent. residue.

Among the constituents of this oil are: linalyl acetate, limonene, dipentene, linalol, and bergaptene.

Bitter Almond Oil.—The volatile oil obtained from the fruit of *Amygdalus communis*. Specific gravity at 15° C., 1.045-1.06; optically inactive; refractive index at 20° C., 1.544-1.545; boiling point, 176-177° C.; soluble in 1 or 1.5 volumes of 70 per cent. alcohol.

The oil consists almost entirely of benzaldehyde which may be estimated by absorption with a hot saturated solution of sodium bisulphite. The chief impurity is prussic acid, which is not always completely removed. This may be readily detected by adding to a small quantity of the oil two or three drops of caustic soda solution, and a few drops of ferrous sulphate solution containing ferric salt. After thoroughly shaking, acidulate with dilute hydrochloric acid, when a blue coloration will be produced if prussic acid is present.

The natural oil may frequently be differentiated from artificial benzaldehyde by the presence of chlorine in the latter. As there is now on the market, however, artificial oil free from chlorine, it is no longer possible, by chemical means, to distinguish with certainty between the natural and the artificial product. To test for chlorine in a sample, a small coil of filter paper, loosely rolled, is saturated with the oil, and burnt in a small porcelain dish, covered with an inverted beaker, the inside of which is moistened with distilled water. When the paper is burnt, the beaker is rinsed with water, filtered, and the filtrate tested for chloride with silver nitrate solution.

Canada snake root oil, from the root of Asarum canadense. Specific gravity at 15° C., 0.940-0.962; optical rotation, slightly lævo-rotatory up to -4°; refractive index at 20° C., 1.485-1.490; saponification number, 100-115; soluble in 3 or 4 volumes of 70 per cent. alcohol.

The principal constituents of the oil are a terpene, asarol alcohol, another alcohol, and methyl eugenol. The oil is too expensive to be used in other than high-class toilet soaps.

Cananga or *Kananga oil*, the earlier distillate from the flowers of Cananga odorata, obtained chiefly from the Philippine Islands. Specific gravity at 15° C., 0.910-0.940; optical rotation, -17° to -30°; refractive index at 20° C., 1.4994-1.5024; esters, calculated as linalyl benzoate, 8-15 per cent.; soluble in 1.5 to 2 volumes of 95 per cent. alcohol, but becoming turbid on further addition.

The oil is qualitatively similar in composition to Ylang-Ylang oil, and contains linalyl benzoate and acetate, esters of geraniol, cadinene, and methyl ester of p-cresol.

Caraway oil, distilled from the seeds of Carum carui. Specific gravity at 15° C., 0.907-0.915; optical rotation, +77° to +79°; refractive index at 20° C., 1.485-1.486; soluble in 3 to 8 volumes of 80 per cent. alcohol. The oil should contain 50-60 per cent. of carvone, which is estimated by absorption with a saturated solution of neutral sodium sulphite. The remainder of the oil consists chiefly of limonene.

Cassia oil, distilled from the leaves of Cinnamomum cassia, and shipped to this country from China in lead receptacles. Specific gravity at 15° C., 1.060-1.068; optical rotation, slightly dextro-rotatory up to +3° 30'; refractive index at 20° C., 1.6014-1.6048; soluble in 3 volumes of 70 per cent. alcohol as a general rule, but occasionally requires 1 to 2 volumes of 80 per cent. alcohol.

The value of the oil depends upon its aldehyde content, the chief constituent being cinnamic aldehyde. This is determined by absorption with a hot saturated solution of sodium bisulphite. Three grades are usually offered, the best containing 80-85 per cent. aldehydes, the second quality, 75-80 per cent., and the lowest grade, 70-75 per cent.

Other constituents of the oil are cinnamyl acetate and cinnamic acid. This oil gives the characteristic odour to Brown Windsor soap, and is useful for sweetening coal-tar medicated soaps.

Cedarwood oil, distilled from the wood of Juniperus virginiana. Specific gravity at 15° C., 0.938-0.960; optical rotation, -35° to -45°; refractive index at 20° C., 1.5013-1.5030. The principal constituents are cedrene and cedrol.

Cinnamon oil, distilled from the bark of Cinnamomum zeylanicum. Specific gravity at 15° C., 1.00-1.035; optical rotation, lævo-rotatory up to -2°; usually soluble in 2 to 3 volumes of 70 per cent. alcohol, but sometimes requires 1 volume of 80 per cent. alcohol for solution; aldehydes, by absorption with sodium bisulphite solution, 55-75 per cent.; and phenols, as measured by absorption with 5 per cent. potash, not exceeding 12 per cent.

The value of this oil is not determined entirely by its aldehyde content as is the case with cassia oil, and any oil containing more than 75 per cent. aldehydes must be regarded with suspicion, being probably admixed with either cassia oil or artificial cinnamic aldehyde. The addition of cinnamon leaf oil which has a specific gravity at 15° C. of 1.044-1.065 is detected by causing a material rise in the proportion of phenols. Besides cinnamic aldehyde the oil contains eugenol and phellandrene.

Citronella Oil.—This oil is distilled from two distinct Andropogon grasses, the Lana Batu and the Maha pangiri, the former being the source of the bulk of Ceylon oil, and the latter being cultivated in the Straits Settlements and Java. The oils from these three localities show well-defined chemical differences.

Ceylon Citronella oil has the specific gravity at 15° C., 0.900-0.920; optical rotation, lævo-rotatory up to -12°; refractive index at 20° C., 1.480-1.484; soluble in 1 volume of 80 per cent. alcohol; total acetylisable constituents, calculated as geraniol, 54-70 per cent.

Singapore Citronella Oil.—Specific gravity at 15° C., 0.890-0.899; optical rotation, usually slightly lævo-rotatory up to -3°; refractive index at 20° C., 1.467-1.471; soluble in 1 to 1.5 volumes of 80 per cent. alcohol; total acetylisable constituents, calculated as geraniol, 80-90 per cent.

Java Citronella Oil.—Specific gravity at 15° C., 0.890-0.901; optical rotation, -1° to -6°; total acetylisable constituents, calculated as geraniol, 75-90 per cent.; soluble in 1-2 volumes of 80 per cent. alcohol.

The chief constituents of the oil are geraniol, citronellal, linalol, borneol, methyl eugenol, camphene, limonene, and dipentene. It is very largely used for perfuming cheap soaps, and also serves as a source for the production of geraniol.

Bois de Rose Femelle oil, or *Cayenne linaloe oil*, distilled from wood of trees of the Burseraceæ species. Specific gravity at 15° C., 0.874-0.880; optical rotation, -11° 30' to -16°; refractive index at 20° C., 1.4608-1.4630; soluble in 1.5 to 2 volumes of 70 per cent. alcohol.

The oil consists almost entirely of linalol, with traces of saponifiable bodies, but appears to be free from methyl heptenone, found by Barbier and Bouveault in Mexican linaloe oil. This oil is distinctly finer in odour than the Mexican product.

Clove oil, distilled from the unripe blossoms of Eugenia caryophyllata, the chief source of which is East Africa (Zanzibar and Pemba). Specific gravity at 15° C., 1.045-

1.061; optical rotation, slightly lævo-rotatory up to -1° 30'; phenols, estimated by absorption with 5 per cent. potash solution, 86-92 per cent.; refractive index at 20° C., 1.5300-1.5360; soluble in 1 to 2 volumes of 70 per cent. alcohol.

The principal constituent of the oil is eugenol, together with caryophyllene and acet-eugenol. While within certain limits the value of this oil is determined by its eugenol content, oils containing more than 93 per cent. phenols are usually less satisfactory in odour, the high proportion of phenols being obtained at the expense of the decomposition of some of the sesquiterpene. Oils with less than 88 per cent. phenols will be found somewhat weak in odour. This oil is extensively used in the cheaper toilet soaps and is an important constituent of carnation soaps. As already mentioned, however, it causes the soap to darken in colour somewhat rapidly, and must not therefore be used in any quantity, except in coloured soaps.

Concrete orris oil, a waxy substance obtained by steam distillation of Florentine orris root.

Melting point, 35-45° C., usually 40-45° C.; free acidity, calculated as myristic acid, 50-80 per cent.; ester, calculated as combined myristic acid, 4-10 per cent.

The greater part of the product consists of the inodorous myristic acid, the chief odour-bearing constituent being irone. The high price of the oil renders its use only possible in the very best quality soaps.

Eucalyptus Oil.—Though there are some hundred or more different oils belonging to this class, only two are of much importance to the soap-maker. These are:—

(i.) Eucalyptus citriodora. Specific gravity at 15° C., 0.870-0.905; optical rotation, slightly dextro-rotatory up to +2°; soluble in 4-5 volumes of 70 per cent. alcohol.

The oil consists almost entirely of citronellic aldehyde, and on absorption with saturated solution of sodium bisulphite should leave very little oil unabsorbed.

(ii.) Eucalyptus globulus, the oil used in pharmacy, and containing 50-65 per cent. cineol. Specific gravity at 15° C., 0.910-0.930; optical rotation, +1° to +10°; soluble in 2 to 3 parts of 70 per cent. alcohol; cineol (estimated by combination with phosphoric acid, pressing, decomposing with hot water, and measuring the liberated cineol), not less than 50 per cent. Besides cineol, the oil contains d-pinene, and valeric, butyric, and caproic aldehydes. It is chiefly used in medicated soaps.

Fennel (sweet) oil, obtained from the fruit of Fœniculum vulgare, grown in Germany, Roumania, and other parts of Europe. Specific gravity at 15° C., 0.965-0.985; optical rotation, +6° to +25°; refractive index at 20° C., 1.515-1.548; usually soluble in 2-6 parts 80 per cent. alcohol, but occasionally requires 1 part of 90 per cent. alcohol.

The chief constituents of the oil are anethol, fenchone, d-pinene, and dipentene.

Geranium oils, distilled from plants of the Pelargonium species. There are three principal kinds of this oil on the market—the African, obtained from Algeria and the neighbourhood, the Bourbon, distilled principally in the Island of Réunion, and the Spanish. The oil is also distilled from plants grown in the South of France, but this oil is not much used by soap-makers. A specially fine article is sold by a few essential oil firms under the name of "Geranium-sur-Rose," which as its name implies, is supposed to be geranium oil distilled over roses. This is particularly suitable for use in high-class soaps. The following are the general properties of these oils. It will be seen that the limits for the figures overlap to a considerable extent.

	African.	Bourbon.	Spanish.	French.
Specific gravity at 15° C.	.890-.900	.888-.895	.895-.898	.897-.900
Optical rotation.	-6° to -10°	-9° to -18°	-8° to -11°	-8° to -11°
Esters, calculated as geranyl tiglate	20-27 per cent.	27-32 per cent.	20-27 per cent.	18-23 per cent.
Total alcohols, as geraniol.	68-75 per cent.	70-80 per cent.	65-75 per cent.	66-75 per cent.
Solubility in 70 per cent. alcohol.	1 in 1.5-2	1 in 1.5-2	1 in 2-3	1 in 1.5-2

The oil contains geraniol and citronellol, both free, and combined with tiglic, valeric, butyric, and acetic acids; also l-menthone. The African and Bourbon varieties are the two most commonly used for soap-perfumery, the Spanish oil being too costly for extensive use.

Ginger-grass oil, formerly regarded as an inferior kind of palma-rosa but now stated to be from an entirely different source. Specific gravity at 15° C., 0.889-0.897; optical rotation, +15°.

The oil contains a large amount of geraniol, together with di-hydrocumin alcohol, d-phellandrene, d-limonene, dipentene, and l-carvone.

Guaiac wood oil, distilled from the wood of Bulnesia sarmienti. Specific gravity at 30° C., 0.967-0.975; optical rotation, -4° 30' to -7°; refractive index at 20° C., 1.506-1.507; soluble in 3 to 5 volumes of 70 per cent. alcohol.

The principal constituent of the oil is guaiac alcohol, or gusiol. This oil, which has what is generally termed a "tea-rose odour," is occasionally used as an adulterant for otto of rose.

Lavender oil, distilled from the flowers of Lavandula vera, grown in England, France, Italy and Spain. The English oil is considerably the most expensive, and is seldom, if ever, used in soap. The French and Italian oils are the most common, the Spanish oil being a comparatively new article, of doubtful botanical origin, and more closely resembling aspic oil.

English Oil.—Specific gravity at 15° C., 0.883-0.900; optical rotation, -4° to -10°; esters, calculated as linalyl acetate, 5-10 per cent.; soluble in 3 volumes of 70 per cent. alcohol.

French and Italian Oils.—Specific gravity at 15° C., 0.885-0.900; optical rotation, -2° to -9°; refractive index at 20° C., 1.459-1.464; esters, calculated as linalyl acetate, 20-40 per cent., occasionally higher; soluble in 1.5-3 volumes of 70 per cent. alcohol.

There was at one time a theory that the higher the proportion of ester the better the oil, but this theory has now to a very large extent become discredited, and there is no doubt that some of the finest oils contain less than 30 per cent. of esters.

Spanish Oil.—Specific gravity at 15° C., 0.900-0.915; optical rotation, -2° to +7°; esters, calculated as linalyl acetate, 2-6 per cent.; soluble in 1-2 volumes of 70 per cent. alcohol.

The chief constituents of lavender oil are linalyl acetate, linalol, geraniol, and linalyl butyrate, while the English oil also contains a distinct amount of cineol.

Lemon oil, prepared by expressing the peel of the nearly ripe fruit of Citrus limonum, and obtained almost entirely from Sicily and Southern Italy. Specific gravity at 15° C., 0.856-0.860; optical rotation, +58° to +63°; refractive index at 20° C., 1.4730-1.4750; aldehydes (citral), 2.5 to 4 per cent.

The principal constituents of the oil are limonene and citral, together with small quantities of pinene, phellandrene, octyl and nonyl aldehydes, citronellal, geraniol, geranyl acetate, and the stearopten, citraptene.

Lemon-grass (so-called *verbena*) oil, distilled from the grass Andropogon citratus, which is grown in India and, more recently, in the West Indies. The oils from these two sources differ somewhat in their properties, and also in value, the former being preferred on account of its greater solubility in alcohol.

East Indian.—Specific gravity at 15° C., 0.898-0.906; optical rotation, -0° 30' to -6°; aldehydes, by absorption with bisulphite of soda solution, 65 to 78 per cent.; refractive index at 20° C., 1.485-1.487; soluble in 2-3 volumes of 70 per cent. alcohol.

West Indian.—Specific gravity at 15° C., 0.886-0.893; optical rotation, faintly lævo-gyrate; refractive index at 20° C., 1.4855-1.4876; soluble in 0.5 volume of 90 per cent. alcohol.

Lime oil, obtained by expression or distillation of the peel of the fruit of Citrus medica, and produced principally in the West Indies.

Expressed Oil.—Specific gravity at 15° C., 0.870-0.885; optical rotation, +38° to +50°. Its most important constituent is citral.

Distilled Oil.—This is entirely different in character to the expressed oil. Its specific gravity at 15° C. is 0.854-0.870; optical rotation, +38° to +54°; soluble in 5-8 volumes of 90 per cent. alcohol.

Linaloe oil, distilled from the wood of trees of the Burseraceæ family, and obtained from Mexico. Specific gravity at 15° C., 0.876-0.892; optical rotation, usually lævo-rotatory, -3° to -13°, but occasionally dextro-rotatory up to +5° 30'; esters, calculated as linalyl acetate, 1-8 per cent.; total alcohols as linalol, determined by acetylation, 54-66 per cent.; soluble in 1-2 volumes of 70 per cent. alcohol.

This oil consists mainly of linalol, together with small quantities of methyl heptenone, geraniol, and d-terpineol.

Marjoram oil, distilled from Origanum majoranoides, and obtained entirely from Cyprus. Specific gravity at 15° C., 0.966; phenols, chiefly carvacrol, estimated by absorption with 5 per cent. caustic potash solution, 80-82 per cent.; soluble in 2-3 volumes of 70 per cent. alcohol.

This oil is used in soap occasionally in place of red thyme oil.

Neroli Bigarade oil, distilled from the fresh blossoms of the bitter orange, Citrus bigaradia. Specific gravity at 15° C., 0.875-0.882; optical rotation, +0° 40' to +10°, and occasionally much higher; refractive index at 20° C., 1.468-1.470; esters, calculated as linalyl acetate, 10-18 per cent.; soluble in 0.75-1.75 volumes of 80 per cent. alcohol, becoming turbid on further addition of alcohol.

The chief constituents of the oil are limonene, linalol, linalyl acetate, geraniol, methyl anthranilate, indol, and neroli camphor.

Orange (sweet) oil, expressed from the peel of Citrus aurantium. Specific gravity at 15° C., 0.849-0.852; optical rotation, +95° to +99°; refractive index at 20° C., 1.4726-1.4732.

The oil contains some 90 per cent. limonene, together with nonyl alcohol, d-linalol, d-terpineol, citral, citronellal, decyl aldehyde, and methyl anthranilate.

Palmarosa, or *East Indian geranium oil,* distilled from Andropogon Schœnanthus, a grass widely grown in India. Specific gravity at 15° C., 0.888-0.895; optical rotation, +1° to -3°; refractive index at 20° C., 1.472-1.476; esters, calculated as linalyl acetate, 7-14 per cent.; total alcohols, as geraniol, 75-93 per cent.; solubility in 70 per cent. alcohol, 1 in 3.

The oil consists chiefly of geraniol, free, and combined with acetic and caproic acids, and dipentene. It is largely used in cheap toilet soaps, particularly in rose soaps. It is also a favourite adulterant for otto of rose, and is used as a source of geraniol.

Patchouli oil, distilled from the leaves of Pogostemon patchouli, a herb grown in India and the Straits Settlements. Specific gravity at 15° C., 0.965-0.990; optical rotation, -45° to -63°; refractive index at 20° C., 1.504-1.511; saponification number, up to 12; sometimes soluble in 0.5 to 1 volume of 90 per cent. alcohol, becoming turbid on further addition. The solubility of the oil in alcohol increases with age. The oil consists to the extent of 97 per cent. of patchouliol and cadinene, which have little influence on its odour, and the bodies responsible for its persistent and characteristic odour have not yet been isolated.

Peppermint oil, distilled from herbs of the Mentha family, the European and American from Mentha piperita, and the

Japanese being generally supposed to be obtained from Mentha arvensis. The locality in which the herb is grown has a considerable influence on the resulting oil, as the following figures show:—

English.—Specific gravity at 15° C., 0.900-0.910; optical rotation, -22° to -33°; total menthol, 55-66 per cent.; free menthol, 50-60 per cent.; soluble in 3-5 volumes of 70 per cent. alcohol.

American.—Specific gravity at 15° C., 0.906-0.920; optical rotation, -20° to -33°; total menthol, 50-60 per cent.; free menthol, 40-50 per cent. The Michigan oil is soluble in 3-5 volumes of 70 per cent. alcohol, but the better Wayne County oil usually requires 1-2 volumes of 80 per cent. alcohol, and occasionally 0.5 volume of 90 per cent. alcohol.

French.—Specific gravity at 15° C., 0.917-0.925; optical rotation, -6° to -10°; total menthol, 45-55 per cent.; free menthol, 35-45 per cent.; soluble in 1 to 1.5 volumes of 80 per cent.

Japanese.—Specific gravity at 25° C., 0.895-0.900; optical rotation, lævo-rotatory up to -43°; solidifies at 17 to 27° C.; total menthol, 70-90 per cent., of which 65-85 per cent. is free; soluble in 3-5 volumes of 70 per cent. alcohol.

The dementholised oil is fluid at ordinary temperatures, has a specific gravity of 0.900-0.906 at 15° C., and contains 50-60 per cent. total menthol.

Some twenty different constituents have been found in American peppermint oil, including menthol, menthone, menthyl acetate, cineol, amyl alcohol, pinene, l-limonene, phellandrene, dimethyl sulphide, menthyl isovalerianate, isovalerianic aldehyde, acetaldehyde, acetic acid, and isovalerianic acid.

Peru balsam oil, the oily portion (so-called "cinnamein") obtained from Peru balsam. Specific gravity at 15° C., 1.100-1.107; optical rotation, slightly dextro-rotatory up to +2°; refractive index at 20° C., 1.569 to 1.576; ester, calculated as benzyl benzoate, 80-87 per cent.; soluble in 1 volume of 90 per cent. alcohol.

The oil consists chiefly of benzyl benzoate and cinnamate, together with styracin, or cinnamyl cinnamate, and a small quantity of free benzoic and cinnamic acids.

Petitgrain oil, obtained by distillation of the twigs and unripe fruit of Citrus bigaradia. There are two varieties of the oil, the French and the South American, the former being the more valuable. Specific gravity at 15° C., 0.886-0.900; optical rotation, -3° to +6°; refractive index at 20° C., 1.4604-1.4650; esters, calculated as linalyl acetate, 40-55 per cent., for the best qualities usually above 50 per cent.; soluble as a rule in 2-3 volumes of 70 per cent. alcohol, but occasionally requires 1-2 volumes of 80 per cent. alcohol.

Among its constituents are limonene, linalyl acetate, geraniol and geranyl acetate.

Pimento oil (allspice), distilled from the fruit of Pimenta officinalis, which is found in the West Indies and Central America. Specific gravity at 15° C., 1.040-1.060; optical rotation, slightly lævo-rotatory up to -4°; refractive index at 20° C., 1.529-1.536; phenols, estimated by absorption with 5 per cent. potash solution, 68-86 per cent.; soluble in 1-2 volumes of 70 per cent. alcohol.

The oil contains eugenol, methyl eugenol, cineol, phellandrene, and caryophyllene.

Rose oil (otto of rose), distilled from the flowers of Rosa damascena, though occasionally the white roses (Rosa alba) are employed. The principal rose-growing district is in Bulgaria, but a small quantity of rose oil is prepared from roses grown in Anatolia, Asia Minor. An opinion as to the purity of otto of rose can only be arrived at after a very full chemical analysis, supplemented by critical examination of its odour by an expert. The following figures, however, will be found to include most oils which can be regarded as genuine. Specific gravity at 30° C., 0.850-0.858; optical rotation at 30° C., -1° 30' to -3°; refractive index at 20° C., 1.4600-1.4645; saponification value, 7-11; solidifying point, 19-22° C.; iodine number, 187-194; stearopten content, 14-20 per cent.; melting point of stearopten, about 32° C.

A large number of constituents have been isolated from otto of rose, many of which are, however, only present in very small quantities. The most important are geraniol, citronellol, phenyl ethyl alcohol, together with nerol, linalol, citral, nonylic aldehyde, eugenol, a sesquiterpene alcohol, and the paraffin stearopten.

Rosemary oil, distilled from the herb Rosemarinus officinalis, and obtained from France, Dalmatia, and Spain. The herb is also grown in England, but the oil distilled therefrom is rarely met with in commerce. The properties of the oils vary with their source, and also with the parts of the plant distilled, distillation of the stalks as well as the leaves tending to reduce the specific gravity and borneol content, and increase the proportion of the lævo-rotatory constituent (lævo-pinene). The following figures may be taken as limits for pure oils:—

French and Dalmatian.—Specific gravity at 15° C., 0.900-0.916; optical rotation, usually dextro-rotatory, up to +15°, but may occasionally be lævo-rotatory, especially if stalks have been distilled with the leaves; ester, calculated as bornyl acetate, 1-6 per cent.; total borneol, 12-18 per cent.; usually soluble in 1-2 volumes of 82.5 per cent. alcohol.

Spanish.—The properties of the Spanish oil are similar to the others, except that it is more frequently lævo-rotatory.

Rosemary oil contains pinene, camphene, cineol, borneol, and camphor.

Sandalwood oil, obtained by distillation of the wood of Santalum album (East Indian), Santalum cygnorum (West Australian), and Amyris balsamifera (West Indian). The oils obtained from these three different sources differ very considerably in value, the East Indian being by far the best.

East Indian.—Specific gravity at 15° C., 0.975-0.980; optical rotation, -14° to -20°; refractive index at 20° C., 1.5045-1.5060; santalol, 92-97 per cent.; usually soluble in 4-6 volumes of 70 per cent. alcohol, though, an old oil occasionally is insoluble in 70 per cent. alcohol.

West Australian.—Specific gravity at 15° C., 0.950-0.968; optical rotation, +5° to +7°; alcohols, calculated as santalol, 73-75 per cent.; insoluble in 70 per cent. alcohol, but readily dissolves in 1-2 volumes of 80 per cent. alcohol.

West Indian.—Specific gravity at 15° C., 0.948-0.967; optical rotation, +13° 30' to +30°; insoluble in 70 per cent. alcohol.

In addition to free santalol, the oil contains esters of santalol and santalal.

Sassafras oil, distilled from the bark of Sassafras officinalis, and obtained chiefly from America. Specific gravity at 15° C., 1.06-1.08; optical rotation, +1° 50' to +4°; refractive index at 20° C., 1.524-1.532; soluble in, 6-10 volumes of 85 per cent. alcohol, frequently soluble in 10-15 volumes of 80 per cent. alcohol.

The chief constituents are safrol, pinene, eugenol, camphor, and phellandrene. The removal of safrol, either intentionally or by accident, owing to cooling of the oil and consequent deposition of the safrol, is readily detected by the reduction of the specific gravity below 1.06.

Thyme oil, red and white, distilled from the green or dried herb, Thymus vulgaris, both French and Spanish oils being met with. These oils are entirely different in character.

French.—Specific gravity at 15° C., 0.91-0.933; slightly lævo-rotatory up to -4°, but usually too dark to observe; phenols, by absorption with 10 per cent. aqueous caustic potash, 25-55 per cent.; refractive index at 20° C., 1.490-1.500; soluble in 1-1.5 volumes of 80 per cent. alcohol.

Spanish.—Specific gravity at 15° C., 0.955-0.966; optical rotation, slightly lævo-gyrate; phenols, 70-80 per cent.; refractive index at 20° C.; 1.5088-1.5122; soluble in 2-3 volumes of 70 per cent. alcohol.

In addition to the phenols, thymol or carvacrol, these oils contain cymene, thymene and pinene.

The white thyme oil is produced by rectifying the red oil, which is generally effected at the expense of a considerable reduction in phenol content, and hence in real odour value of the oil.

Verbena Oil.—The oil usually sold under this name is really lemon-grass oil (which see *supra*). The true verbena oil or French verveine is, however, occasionally met with. This is distilled in France from the verbena officinalis, and has the following properties: Specific gravity at 15° C., 0.891-0.898; optical rotation, slightly dextro- or lævo-rotatory; aldehydes, 70-75 per cent.; soluble in 2 volumes of 70 per cent. alcohol.

The oil contains citral.

Vetivert oil, distilled from the grass, Andropogon muricatus, or Cus Cus, and grown in the East Indies.

Specific gravity at 15° C., 1.01-1.03; optical rotation, +20° to +26°; saponification number, 15-30; refractive index at 20° C., 1.521-1.524; soluble in 2 volumes of 80 per cent. alcohol.

The price of this oil makes its use prohibitive except in the highest class soaps.

Wintergreen Oil.—There are two natural sources of this oil, the Gaultheria procumbens and the Betula lenta. Both oils consist almost entirely of methyl salicylate and are practically identical in properties, the chief difference being that the former has a slight lævo-rotation, while the latter is inactive.

Specific gravity at 15° C., 1.180-1.187; optical rotation, Gaultheria oil, up to -1°, Betula oil, inactive; ester as methyl salicylate, at least 98 per cent.; refractive index at 20° C., 1.5354-1.5364; soluble in 2-6 volumes of 70 per cent. alcohol.

Besides methyl salicylate, the oil contains triaconitane, an aldehyde or ketone, and an alcohol.

Ylang-ylang oil, distilled from the flowers of Cananga odorata, the chief sources being the Philippine Islands and Java. Specific gravity at 15° C., 0.924-0.950; optical rotation, -30° to -60°, and occasionally higher; refractive index at 20° C., 1.496-1.512; ester, calculated as linalyl benzoate, 27-45 per cent., occasionally up to 50 per cent.; usually soluble in 1/2 volume of 90 per cent. alcohol.

The composition of the oil is qualitatively the same as that of Cananga oil, but it is considerably more expensive and therefore can only be used in the highest grade soaps.

Artificial and Synthetic Perfumes.

During the past few years the constitution of essential oils has been studied by a considerable number of chemists, and the composition of many oils has been so fully determined that very good imitations can often be made at cheaper prices than those of the genuine oils, rendering it possible to produce cheap soaps having perfumes which were formerly only possible in the more expensive article.

There is a considerable distinction, however, often lost sight of, between an *artificial* and a *synthetic* oil. An artificial oil may be produced by separating various constituents from certain natural oils, and so blending these, with or without the addition of other substances, as to produce a desired odour, the perfume being, at any rate in part, obtained from natural oils. A synthetic perfume, on the other hand, is entirely the product of the chemical laboratory, no natural oil or substance derived therefrom entering into its composition.

The following are among the most important bodies of this class:—

Amyl salicylate, the ester prepared from amyl alcohol and salicylic acid, sometimes known as "Orchidée" or "Trèfle". This is much used for the production of a clover-scented soap. It has the specific gravity at 15° C., 1.052-1.054; optical rotation, +1° 16' to +1° 40'; refractive index at 20° C., 1.5056; and should contain not less than 97 per cent. ester, calculated as amyl salicylate.

Anisic aldehyde, or *aubépine*, prepared by oxidation of anethol, and possessing a pleasant, hawthorn odour. This has the specific gravity at 15° C., 1.126; refractive index at 20° C., 1.5693; is optically inactive, and dissolves readily in one volume of 70 per cent. alcohol.

Benzyl Acetate, the ester obtained from benzyl alcohol and acetic acid. This has a very strong and somewhat coarse, penetrating odour, distinctly resembling jasmine. Its specific gravity at 15° C. is 1.062-1.065; refractive index at 20° C., 1.5020; and it should contain at least 97-98 per cent. ester, calculated as benzyl acetate.

Citral, the aldehyde occurring largely in lemon-grass and verbena oils, also to a less extent in lemon and orange oils, and possessing an intense lemon-like odour. It has a specific gravity at 15° C., 0.896-0.897, is optically inactive, and should be entirely absorbed by a hot saturated solution of sodium bisulphite.

Citronellal, an aldehyde possessing the characteristic odour of citronella oil, in which it occurs to the extent of about 20 per cent., and constituting considerably over 90 per cent. of eucalyptus citriodora oil. Its specific gravity at 15° C. is 0.862; refractive index at 20° C., 1.447; optical rotation, +8° to +12°; and it should be entirely absorbed by a hot saturated solution of sodium bisulphite.

Coumarin, a white crystalline product found in Tonka beans, and prepared synthetically from salicylic acid. It has an odour resembling new-mown hay, and melts at 67° C.

Geraniol, a cyclic alcohol, occurring largely in geranium, palma-rosa, and citronella oils. Its specific gravity at 15° C. is 0.883-0.885; refractive index at 20° C., 1.4762-1.4770; it is optically inactive, and boils at 218°-225° C.

Heliotropin, which possesses the characteristic odour of heliotrope, is prepared artificially from safrol. It crystallises in small prisms melting at 86° C.

Hyacinth.—Most of the articles sold under this name are secret blends of the different makers. Styrolene has an odour very much resembling hyacinth, and probably forms the basis of most of these preparations, together with terpineol, and other artificial bodies. The properties of the oil vary considerably for different makes.

Ionone, a ketone first prepared by Tiemann, and having when diluted a pronounced violet odour. It is prepared by treating a mixture of citral and acetone with barium hydrate, and distilling in vacuo. Two isomeric ketones, α-ionone and β-ionone, are produced, the article of commerce being usually a mixture of both. The two ketones have the following properties:—

Alpha-ionone.—Specific gravity at 15° C., 0.9338; refractive index at 16.5 C., 1.50048 (Chuit); optically it is inactive.

Beta-ionone.—Specific gravity at 15° C., 0.9488; refractive index at 16.8° C., 1.52070 (Chuit); optically it is inactive also.

The product is usually sold in 10 or 20 per cent. alcoholic solution ready for use.

Jasmine.—This is one of the few cases in which the artificial oil is probably superior to that obtained from the natural flowers, possibly due to the extreme delicacy of the odour, and its consequent slight decomposition during preparation from the flowers. The chemical composition of the floral perfume has been very exhaustively studied, and the artificial article now on the market may be described as a triumph of synthetical chemistry. Among its constituents are benzyl acetate, linalyl acetate, benzyl alcohol, indol, methyl anthranilate, and a ketone jasmone.

Linalol, the alcohol forming the greater part of linaloe and bois de rose oils, and found also in lavender, neroli, petitgrain, bergamot, and many other oils. The article has the specific gravity at 15° C., 0.870-0.876; optical rotation, -12° to -14°; refractive index at 20° C., 1.463-1.464; and when estimated by acetylation, yields about 70 per cent. of alcohols.

Linalyl acetate, or *artificial bergamot oil*, is the ester formed when linalol is treated with acetic anhydride. It possesses a bergamot-like odour, but it is doubtful whether its value is commensurate with its greatly increased price over that of ordinary bergamot oil. It has the specific gravity at 15° C., 0.912.

Musk (Artificial).—Several forms of this are to be obtained, practically all of which are nitro-derivatives of aromatic hydrocarbons. The original patent of Baur, obtained in 1889, covered the tri-nitro-derivative of tertiary butyl xylene. The melting point of the pure article usually lies between 108° and 112° C., and the solubility in 95 per cent. alcohol ranges from 1 in 120 to 1 in 200, though more soluble forms are also made.

An important adulterant, which should always be tested for, is acetanilide (antifebrin), which may be detected by the characteristic isocyanide odour produced when musk containing this substance is boiled with alcoholic potash, and a few drops of chloroform added. Acetanilide also increases the solubility in 95 per cent. alcohol.

Neroli Oil (Artificial).—Like jasmine oil, the chemistry of neroli oil is now very fully known, and it is therefore possible to prepare an artificial product which is a very good approximation to the natural oil, and many such are now on the market, which, on account of their comparative cheapness, commend themselves to the soap-perfumer. These consist chiefly of linalol, geraniol, linalyl acetate, methyl anthranilate, and citral.

Mirbane Oil or *Nitrobenzene.*—This is a cheap substitute for oil of bitter almonds, or benzaldehyde, and is a very coarse, irritating perfume, only suitable for use in the very cheapest soaps. It is prepared by the action of a mixture of nitric and sulphuric acids on benzene at a temperature not exceeding 40° C. Its specific gravity is 1.205-1.206; refractive index at 20° C., 1.550; and boiling point, 206° C.

Niobe oil, or *ethyl benzoate*, the ester obtained from ethyl alcohol and benzoic acid, and having the specific gravity at 15° C., 1.094-1.095; refractive index at 20° C., 1.5167; boiling point, 196.5°-198° C.; soluble in 1.5 volumes of 70 per cent. alcohol.

Oeillet is a combination possessed of a sweet carnation-like odour and having as a basis, eugenol or isoeugenol. Its properties vary with the source of supply.

Rose Oil (Artificial).—Several good and fairly cheap artificial rose oils are now obtainable, consisting chiefly of citronellol, geraniol, linalol, phenyl ethyl alcohol, and citral. In some cases stearopten or other wax is added, to render the oil more similar in appearance to the natural article, but as these are inodorous, no advantage is gained in this way, and there is, further, the inconvenience in cold weather of having to first melt the oil before use.

Safrol, an ether which is the chief constituent of sassafras oil, and also found in considerable quantity in camphor oil. It is sold as an artificial sassafras oil, and is very much used in perfuming cheap toilet or household soaps. Its specific gravity at 15° C. is 1.103-1.106; refractive index at 20° C.,

1.5373; and it dissolves in fifteen volumes of 80 per cent. alcohol.

Santalol, the alcohol or mixture of alcohols obtained from sandalwood oil. Its specific gravity at 15° C. is 0.9795; optical rotation, -18°; and refractive index at 20° C., 1.507.

Terebene, a mixture of dipentene and other hydrocarbons prepared from turpentine oil by treatment with concentrated sulphuric acid, is used chiefly in medicated soaps. Its specific gravity at 15° C. is 0.862-0.868; the oil is frequently slightly dextro- or lævo-rotatory; the refractive index at 20° C., 1.470-1.478.

Terpineol, an alcohol also prepared from turpentine oil by the action of sulphuric acid, terpene hydrate being formed as an intermediate substance. It has a distinctly characteristic lilac odour, and on account of its cheapness is much used in soap perfumery, especially for a lilac or lily soap. Its specific gravity at 15° C. is 0.936-0.940; refractive index at 20° C., 1.4812-1.4835; and boiling point about 210°-212° C. It is optically inactive, and readily soluble in 1.5 volumes of 70 per cent. alcohol.

Vanillin, a white crystalline solid, melting at 80°-82° C. and prepared by the oxidation of isoeugenol. It has a strong characteristic odour, and occurs, associated with traces of benzoic acid and heliotropin, in the vanilla bean. It can only be used in small quantity in light-coloured soaps, as it quickly tends to darken the colour of the soap.

CHAPTER IX.

GLYCERINE MANUFACTURE AND PURIFICATION.

Treatment of Lyes—Evaporation to Crude Glycerine—Distillation—Distilled and Dynamite Glycerine—Chemically Pure Glycerine—Animal Charcoal for Decolorisation—Glycerine obtained by other Methods of Saponification—Yield of Glycerine from Fats and Oils.

As pointed out in Chapter II. the fatty acids, which, combined with soda or potash, form soap, occur in nature almost invariably in the form of glycerides, *i.e.*, compounds of fatty acids with glycerol, and as the result of saponification of a fat or oil glycerine is set free.

In Chapter V. processes of soap-making are described in which (1) the glycerine is retained in the finished soap, and (2) the glycerine is contained in the lyes, in very dilute solution, contaminated with salt and other impurities. These lyes, though now constituting the chief source of profit in the manufacture of cheap soaps, were till early in last century simply run down the drains as waste liquor.

Much attention has been devoted to the purification and concentration of glycerine lyes; and elaborate plant of various forms has been devised for the purpose.

Treatment of Lyes.—The spent lyes withdrawn from the soap-pans are cooled, and the soap, which has separated during the cooling, is carefully removed and returned to the soap-house for utilisation in the manufacture of brown soap. Spent lyes may vary in their content of glycerol from 3 to 8 per cent., and this depends not only upon the system adopted in the working of the soap-pans, but also upon the materials used. Although, in these days of pure caustic soda, spent lyes are more free from impurities than formerly, the presence of sulphides and sulphites should be carefully avoided, if it is desired to produce good glycerine.

The lyes are transferred to a lead-lined tank of convenient size, and treated with commercial hydrochloric acid and aluminium sulphate, sufficient being added of the former to neutralise the free alkali, and render the liquor faintly acid, and of the latter to completely precipitate the fatty acids. The acid should be run in slowly, and the point when enough has been added, is indicated by blue litmus paper being slightly reddened by the lyes.

The whole is then agitated with air, when a sample taken from the tank and filtered should give a clear filtrate.

Having obtained this clear solution, agitation is stopped, and the contents of the tank passed through a filter press. The scum, which accumulates on the treatment tank, may be transferred to a perforated box suspended over the tank, and the liquor allowed to drain from it. The filtered liquor is now rendered slightly alkaline by the addition of caustic soda or carbonate, and, after filtering, is ready for evaporation.

The acid and alum salt used in the above treatment must be carefully examined for the presence of arsenic, and any deliveries of either article, which contain that impurity, rejected.

Lime, bog ore, and various metallic salts, such as ferric chloride, barium chloride, and copper sulphate have been suggested, and in some instances are used instead of aluminium sulphate, but the latter is generally employed.

Evaporation to Crude Glycerine.—The clear treated lyes, being now free from fatty, resinous, and albuminous matter, and consisting practically of an aqueous solution of common salt (sodium chloride) and glycerine, is converted into crude glycerine by concentration, which eliminates the water and causes most of the salt to be deposited.

This concentration was originally performed in open pans heated by fire or waste combustible gases. In the bottom of each pan was placed a dish in which the salt deposited, and this dish was lifted out periodically by the aid of an overhead crane and the contents emptied and washed. Concentration was continued until the temperature of the liquor was 300° F. (149° C.), when it was allowed to rest before storing.

This liquor on analysis gave 80 per cent. glycerol and from 9 to 10-1/2 per cent. salts (ash); hence the present standard for crude glycerine.

Concentration in open pans has now been superseded by evaporation *in vacuo*. The subject of the gradual development of the modern efficient evaporating plant from the vacuum pan, originated and successfully applied by Howard in 1813 in the sugar industry, is too lengthy to detail here, suffice it to say that the multiple effects now in vogue possess distinct advantages—the greatest of these being increased efficiency combined with economy.

The present type of evaporator consists of one or more vessels, each fitted with a steam chamber through which are fixed vertical hollow tubes. The steam chamber of the first vessel is heated with direct steam, or with exhaust steam (supplied from the exhaust steam receiver into which passes the waste steam of the factory); the treated lyes circulating through the heated tubes is made to boil at a lower temperature, with the reduced pressure, than is possible by heating in open pans.

The vapour given off by the boiling liquor is conveyed through large pipes into the steam chamber of the second vessel, where its latent heat is utilised in producing evaporation, the pressure being further reduced, as this second vessel is under a greater vacuum than No. 1. Thus we get a "double effect," as the plant consisting of two pans is termed. The vapours discharged from the second vessel during boiling are passed through pipes to the steam chamber of the third vessel (in a "triple effect"), and there being condensed, create a partial vacuum in the second vessel. The third vessel may also be heated by means of live steam. The vapours arising from the last vessel of the evaporating plant, or in the case of a "single effect" from the vessel, are conveyed into a condenser and condensed by injection water, which is drawn off by means of the pump employed for maintaining a vacuum of 28 inches in the vessel.

In the most recent designs of large evaporative installations, the vapours generated from the last vessel are drawn through a device consisting of a number of tubes enclosed in a casing, and the latent heat raises the temperature of the treated lyes proceeding through the tubes to supply the evaporator.

It will thus be observed that the object of multiple effects is to utilise all the available heat in performing the greatest possible amount of work. Special devices are attached to the plant for automatically removing the condensed water from the steam chambers without the loss of useful heat, and as a precaution against splashing over and subsequent loss of glycerine through conveyance to the steam chamber, dash plates and "catch-alls" or "save-alls" of various designs are fitted on each vessel.

In working the plant, the liquor in each vessel is kept at a fairly constant level by judicious feeding from one to the other; the first vessel is, of course, charged with treated lyes. As the liquor acquires a density of 42° Tw. (25° B.) salt begins to deposit, and may be withdrawn into one of the many patented appliances, in which it is freed from glycerine, washed and dried ready for use at the soap pans. Difficulty is sometimes experienced with the tubes becoming choked with salt, thereby diminishing and retarding evaporation. It may be necessary to dissolve the encrusted salt with lyes or water, but with careful working the difficulty can be obviated by washing out with weak lyes after each batch of crude glycerine has been run away, or by increasing the circulation.

It is claimed that by the use of the revolving heater designed by Lewkowitsch, the salting up of tubes is prevented.

The salt having been precipitated and removed, evaporation is continued until a sample taken from the last vessel has a density of 60° Tw. (33.3 B.) at 60° F. (15.5° C.). When this point is reached, the crude glycerine is ready to be withdrawn into a tank, and, after allowing the excess of salt to deposit, may be transferred to the storage tank.

The colour of crude glycerine varies from light brown to dark brown, almost black, and depends largely on the materials used for soap-making. The organic matter present in good crude glycerine is small in amount, often less than 1 per cent.; arsenic, sulphides and sulphites should be absent. Crude glycerine is refined in some cases by the producers themselves; others sell it to firms engaged more particularly in the refined glycerine trade.

Distillation.—Crude glycerine is distilled under vacuum with the aid of superheated steam. The still is heated directly with a coal or coke fire, and in this fire space is the superheater, which consists of a coil of pipes through which high pressure steam from the boiler is superheated.

The distillation is conducted at a temperature of 356°F. (180° C.). To prevent the deposition and burning of salt on the still-bottom during the distillation, a false bottom is supported about 1 foot from the base of the still. With the same object in view, it has been suggested to rotate the contents with an agitator fixed in the still.

Every care is taken that the still does not become overheated; this precaution not only prevents loss of glycerine through carbonisation, but also obviates the production of tarry and other bodies which might affect the colour, taste, and odour of the distilled glycerine. The vacuum to be used will, of course, depend upon the heat of the fire and still, but as a general rule good results are obtained with an 18 inch vacuum.

There are quite a large number of designs for still heads, and "catch-alls," having for their object the prevention of loss of glycerine.

The distillate passes into a row of condensers, to each of which is attached a receptacle or receiver. It is needless to state that the condensing capacity should be in excess of theoretical requirements. The fractions are of varying strengths and quality; that portion, with a density less than 14° Tw. (19.4° B.), is returned to the treated-lyes tank. The other portion of the distillate is concentrated by means of a dry steam coil in a suitable vessel under a 28 inch vacuum.

When sufficiently concentrated the glycerine may be decolorised, if necessary, by treating with 1 per cent. animal charcoal and passing through a filter press, from which it issues as "dynamite glycerine".

The residue in the still, consisting of 50-60 per cent. glycerine and varying proportions of various sodium salts—*e.g.* acetate, chloride, sulphate, and combinations with non-volatile organic acids—is generally boiled with water and treated with acid.

The tar, which is separated, floats on the surface as the liquor is cooling, and may be removed by ladles, or the whole mixed with waste charcoal, and filtered.

The filtrate is then evaporated, when the volatile organic acids are driven off; the concentrated liquor is finally mixed with crude glycerine which is ready for distillation, or it may be distilled separately.

Distilled Glycerine.—This class of commercial glycerine, although of limited use in various other branches of industry, finds its chief outlet in the manufacture of explosives.

Specifications are usually given in contracts drawn up between buyers and sellers, to which the product must conform.

The chief stipulation for dynamite glycerine is its behaviour in the nitration test. When glycerine is gradually added to a cold mixture of strong nitric and sulphuric acids, it is converted into nitro-glycerine, which separates as an oily layer on the surface of the acid. The more definite and rapid the separation, the more suitable is the glycerine for dynamite-making.

Dynamite glycerine should be free from arsenic, lime, chlorides, and fatty acids, the inorganic matter should not amount to more than 0.1 per cent., and a portion diluted and treated with nitrate of silver solution should give no turbidity or discoloration in ten minutes. The specific gravity should be 1.262 at 15° C. (59° F.) and the colour somewhat yellow.

Chemically pure glycerine or double distilled glycerine is produced by redistilling "once distilled" glycerine. Every care is taken to avoid all fractions which do not withstand the nitrate of silver test. The distillation is very carefully performed under strict supervision.

The distillate is concentrated and after treatment with animal charcoal and filtration should conform to the requirements of the British Pharmacopœia. These are specified as follows: Specific gravity at 15.5° C., 1.260. It should yield no characteristic reaction with the tests for lead, copper, arsenium, iron, calcium, potassium, sodium, ammonium, chlorides, or sulphates. It should contain no sugars and leave no residue on burning.

Animal Charcoal for Decolorisation.—The application of animal charcoal for decolorising purposes dates back a century, and various are the views that have been propounded to explain its action. Some observers base it upon the physical condition of the so-called carbon present, and no doubt this is an important factor, coupled with the porosity. Others consider that the nitrogen, which is present in all animal charcoal and extremely difficult to remove, is essential to the action. Animal charcoal should be freed from gypsum (sulphate of lime), lest in the burning, sulphur compounds be formed which would pass into the glycerine and contaminate it.

The "char" should be well boiled with water, then carbonate of soda or caustic soda added in sufficient quantity to give an alkaline reaction, and again well boiled. The liquor is withdrawn and the charcoal washed until the washings are no longer alkaline. The charcoal is then separated from the liquor and treated with hydrochloric acid; opinions differ as to the amount of acid to be used. Some contend that phosphate of lime plays such an important part in decolorising that it should not be removed, but it has, however, been demonstrated that this substance after exposure to heat has very little decolorising power.

Animal charcoal boiled with four times its weight of a mixture consisting of equal parts of commercial hydrochloric acid (free from arsenic) and water for twelve hours, then washed free from acid, dried, and burned in closed vessels gives a product possessed of great decolorising power for use with glycerines.

A good animal charcoal will have a dull appearance, and be of a deep colour; it should be used in fine grains and not in the form of a powder.

The charcoal from the filter presses is washed free from glycerine (which is returned to the treated lyes), cleansed from foreign substances by the above treatment and revivified by carefully heating in closed vessels for twelve hours.

Glycerine obtained by other Methods of Saponification.— French saponification or "candle crude" glycerine is the result of concentration of "sweet water" produced in the manufacture of stearine and by the autoclave process. It contains 85-90 per cent. glycerol, possesses a specific gravity of 1.240-1.242, and may be readily distinguished from the soap-crude glycerine by the absence of salt (sodium chloride). This glycerine is easily refined by treatment with charcoal.

The glycerine water resulting from acid saponification methods requires to be rendered alkaline by the addition of lime—the sludge is separated, and the liquor evaporated to crude. The concentration may be performed in two stages—first to a density of 32° Tw. (20° B.), when the calcium sulphate is allowed to deposit, and the separated liquor concentrated to 48° Tw. (28° B.) glycerine, testing 85 per cent. glycerol and upwards.

Yield of Glycerine from Fats and Oils.—The following represent practicable results which should be obtained from the various materials:—

Tallow	9	per cent. of 80 per cent. Glycerol.
Cotton-seed oil	10	"
Cocoa-nut oil	12	"
Palm-kernel oil	18	"
Olive oil	10	"
Palm oil	6	"
Greases (Bone fats)	6-8	"

The materials vary in glycerol content with the methods of preparation; especially is this the case with tallows and greases.

Every care should be taken that the raw materials are fresh and they should be carefully examined to ascertain if any decomposition has taken place in the glycerides—this would be denoted by the presence of an excess of free acidity, and the amount of glycerol obtainable from such a fat would be correspondingly reduced.

CHAPTER X.

ANALYSIS OF RAW MATERIALS, SOAP, AND GLYCERINE.

Fats and Oils—Alkalies and Alkali Salts—Essential Oils—Soap—Lyes—Crude Glycerine.

Raw Materials.—Average figures have already been given in Chapters III. and VIII. for the more important physical and chemical characteristics of fats and oils, also of essential oils; the following is an outline of the processes usually adopted in their determination. For fuller details, text-books dealing exhaustively with the respective subjects should be consulted.

FATS AND OILS.

It is very undesirable that any of these materials should be allowed to enter the soap pan without an analysis having first been made, as the oil may not only have become partially hydrolysed, involving a loss of glycerine, or contain albuminous matter rendering the soap liable to develop rancidity, but actual sophistication may have taken place. Thus a sample of tallow recently examined by the authors contained as much as 40 per cent. of an unsaponifiable wax, which would have led to disaster in the soap pan, had the bulk been used without examination. After observing the appearance, colour, and odour of the sample, noting any characteristic feature, the following physical and chemical data should be determined.

Specific Gravity at 15° C. This may be taken by means of a Westphal balance, or by using a picnometer of either the ordinary gravity bottle shape, with perforated stopper, or the Sprengel U-tube. The picnometer should be calibrated with distilled water at 15° C. The specific gravity of solid fats may be taken at an elevated temperature, preferably that of a boiling water bath.

Free acidity is estimated by weighing out from 2 to 5 grammes of the fat or oil, dissolving in neutral alcohol (purified methylated spirit) with gentle heat, and titrating with a standard aqueous or alcoholic solution of caustic soda or potash, using phenol-phthalein as indicator.

The contents of the flask are well shaken after each addition of alkali, and the reaction is complete when the slight excess of alkali causes a permanent pink coloration with the indicator. The standard alkali may be N/2, N/5, or N/10.

It is usual to calculate the result in terms of oleic acid (1 c.c. N/10 alkali = 0.0282 gramme oleic acid), and express in percentage on the fat or oil.

Example.—1.8976 grammes were taken, and required 5.2 c.c. of N/10 KOH solution for neutralisation.

$$\frac{5.2 \times 0.0282 \times 100}{1.8976} = 7.72 \text{ per cent. free fatty acids, expressed as oleic acid.}$$

The free acidity is sometimes expressed as *acid value*, which is the amount of KOH in milligrammes necessary to neutralise the free acid in 1 gramme of fat or oil.

In the above example:—

$$\frac{5.2 \times 5.61}{} = 15.3 \text{ acid value.}$$

1.8976

The *saponification equivalent* is determined by weighing 2-4 grammes of fat or oil into a wide-necked flask (about 250 c.c. capacity), adding 30 c.c. neutral alcohol, and warming under a reflux condenser on a steam or water-bath. When boiling, the flask is disconnected, 50 c.c. of an approximately semi-normal alcoholic potash solution carefully added from a burette, together with a few drops of phenol-phthalein solution, and the boiling under a reflux condenser continued, with frequent agitation, until saponification is complete (usually from 30-60 minutes) which is indicated by the absence of fatty globules. The excess of alkali is titrated with N/1 hydrochloric or sulphuric acid.

The value of the approximately N/2 alkali solution is ascertained by taking 50 c.c. together with 30 c.c. neutral alcohol in a similar flask, boiling for the same length of time as the fat, and titrating with N/1 hydrochloric or sulphuric acid. The "saponification equivalent" is the amount of fat or oil in grammes saponified by 1 equivalent or 56.1 grammes of caustic potash.

Example.—1.8976 grammes fat required 18.95 c.c. N/1 acid to neutralise the unabsorbed alkali.

Fifty c.c. approximately N/2 alcoholic potash solution required 25.6 c.c. N/ acid..

25.6 - 18.95 = 6.65 c.c. N/1 KOH required by fat.

1.8976 × 1000 / 6.65 = 285.3 Saponification Equivalent.

The result of this test is often expressed as the "Saponification Value," which is the number of milligrammes of KOH required for the saponification of 1 gramme of fat. This may be found by dividing 56,100 by the saponification equivalent or by multiplying the number of c.c. of N/1 alkali absorbed, by 56.1 and dividing by the quantity of fat taken. Thus, in the above example:—

6.65 × 56.1 / 1.8976 = 196.6 Saponification Value.

The *ester* or *ether value*, or number of milligrammes of KOH required for the saponification of the neutral esters or glycerides in 1 gramme of fat, is represented by the difference between the saponification and acid values. In the example given, the ester value would be 196.6 - 15.3 = 181.3.

Unsaponifiable Matter.—The usual method adopted is to saponify about 5 grammes of the fat or oil with 50 c.c. of approximately N/2 alcoholic potash solution by boiling under a reflux condenser with frequent agitation for about 1 hour. The solution is then evaporated to dryness in a porcelain basin over a steam or water-bath, and the resultant soap dissolved in about 200 c.c. hot water. When sufficiently cool, the soap solution is transferred to a separating funnel, 50 c.c. of ether added, the whole well shaken, and allowed to rest. The ethereal layer is removed to another separator, more ether being added to the aqueous soap solution, and again separated. The two ethereal extracts are then washed with water to deprive them of any soap, separated, transferred to a flask, and the ether distilled off upon a water-bath. The residue, dried in the oven at 100° C. until constant, is the "unsaponifiable matter," which is calculated to per cent. on the oil.

In this method, it is very frequently most difficult to obtain a distinct separation of ether and aqueous soap solution—an intermediate layer of emulsion remaining even after prolonged standing, and various expedients have been recommended to overcome this, such as addition of alcohol (when petroleum ether is used), glycerine, more ether, water, or caustic potash solution, or by rotatory agitation.

A better plan is to proceed as in the method above described as far as dissolving the resulting soap in 200 c.c. water, and then boil for twenty or thirty minutes. Slightly cool and acidify with dilute sulphuric acid (1 to 3), boil until the fatty acids are clear, wash with hot water free from mineral acid, and dry by filtering through a hot water funnel.

Two grammes of the fatty acids are now dissolved in neutral alcohol saturated with some solvent, preferably a light fraction of benzoline, a quantity of the solvent added to take up the unsaponifiable matter, and the whole boiled under a reflux condenser. After cooling, the liquid is titrated with N/2 aqueous KOH solution, using phenolphthalein as indicator, this figure giving the amount of the total fatty acids present. The whole is then poured into a separating funnel, when separation immediately takes place. The alcoholic layer is withdrawn, the benzoline washed with warm water (about 32° C.) followed by neutral alcohol (previously saturated with the solvent), and transferred to a tared flask, which is attached to a condenser, and the benzoline distilled off. The last traces of solvent remaining in the flask are removed by gently warming in the water-oven, and the flask cooled and weighed, thus giving the amount of unsaponifiable matter.

Constitution of the Unsaponifiable Matter.— Unsaponifiable matter may consist of cholesterol, phytosterol, solid alcohols (cetyl and ceryl alcohols), or hydrocarbons (mineral oil). Cholesterol is frequently found in animal fats, and phytosterol is a very similar substance present in vegetable fats. Solid alcohols occur naturally in sperm oil, but hydrocarbons, which may be generally recognised by the fluorescence or bloom they give to the oil, are not natural constituents of animal or vegetable oils and fats.

The presence of cholesterol and phytosterol may be detected by dissolving a small portion of the unsaponifiable matter in acetic anhydride, and adding a drop of the solution to one drop of 50 per cent. sulphuric acid on a spot plate, when a characteristic blood red to violet coloration is produced. It has been proposed to differentiate between cholesterol and phytosterol by their melting points, but it is more reliable to compare the crystalline forms, the former crystallising in laminæ, while the latter forms groups of needle-shaped tufts. Another method is to convert the substance into acetate, and take its melting point, cholesterol acetate melting at 114.3-114.8° C., and phytosterol acetate at 125.6°-137° C.

Additional tests for cholesterol have been recently proposed by Lifschütz (*Ber. Deut. Chem. Ges.*, 1908, 252-255), and Golodetz (*Chem. Zeit.*, 1908, 160). In that due to the former, which depends on the oxidation of cholesterol to oxycholesterol ester and oxycholesterol, a few milligrammes of the substance are dissolved in 2-3 c.c. glacial acetic acid, a little benzoyl peroxide added, and the solution boiled, after which four drops of strong sulphuric acid are added, when a violet-blue or green colour is produced, if cholesterol is present, the violet colour being due to oxycholesterol ester, the green to oxycholesterol. Two tests are suggested by Golodetz (1) the addition of one or two drops of a reagent consisting of five parts of concentrated sulphuric acid and three parts of formaldehyde solution, which colours cholesterol a blackish-brown, and (2) the addition of one drop of 30 per cent. formaldehyde solution to a solution of the substance in trichloracetic acid, when with cholesterol an intense blue coloration is produced.

Water.—From 5 to 20 grammes of the fat or oil are weighed into a tared porcelain or platinum dish, and stirred with a thermometer, whilst being heated over a gas flame at 100° C. until bubbling or cracking has ceased, and reweighed, the loss in weight representing the water. In cases of spurting a little added alcohol will carry the water off quietly.

To prevent loss by spurting, Davis (*J. Amer. Chem. Soc.*, 23, 487) has suggested that the fat or oil should be added to a previously dried and tared coil of filter paper contained in a stoppered weighing bottle, which is then placed in the oven and dried at 100° C. until constant in weight. Of course, this method is not applicable to oils or fats liable to oxidation on heating.

Dregs, Dirt, Adipose Tissue, Fibre, etc.—From 10 to 15 grammes of the fat are dissolved in petroleum ether with frequent stirring, and passed through a tared filter paper. The residue retained by the filter paper is washed with petroleum ether until free from fat, dried in the water-oven at 100° C. and weighed.

If the amount of residue is large, it may be ignited, and the proportion and nature of the ash determined.

The amount of impurities may also be estimated by Tate's method, which is performed by weighing 5 grammes of fat into a separating funnel, dissolving in ether, and allowing the whole to stand to enable the water to deposit. After six hours' rest the water is withdrawn, the tube of the separator carefully dried, and the ethereal solution filtered through a dried tared filter paper into a tared flask. Well wash the filter with ether, and carefully dry at 100° C. The ether in the flask is recovered, and the flask dried until all ether is expelled, and its weight is constant. The amount of fat in the flask gives the quantity of actual fat in the sample taken; the loss represents the water and other impurities, and these latter may be obtained from the increase of weight of the filter paper.

Starch may be detected by the blue coloration it gives with iodine solution, and confirmed by microscopical examination, or it may be converted into glucose by inversion, and the glucose estimated by means of Fehling's solution.

Iodine Absorption.—This determination shows the amount of iodine absorbed by a fat or oil, and was devised by Hübl, the reagents required being as follows:—

(1) Solution of 25 grammes iodine in 500 c.c. absolute alcohol; (2) solution of 30 grammes mercuric chloride in 500 c.c. absolute alcohol, these two solutions being mixed together and allowed to stand at least twelve hours before use; (3) a freshly prepared 10 per cent. aqueous solution of potassium iodide; and (4) a N/10 solution of sodium thiosulphate, standardised just prior to use by titrating a weighed quantity of resublimed iodine dissolved in potassium iodide solution.

In the actual determination, 0.2 to 0.5 gramme of fat or fatty acids is carefully weighed into a well-fitting stoppered 250 c.c. bottle, dissolved in 10 c.c. chloroform, and 25 c.c. of the Hübl reagent added, the stopper being then moistened with potassium iodide solution and placed firmly in the bottle, which is allowed to stand at rest in a dark place for four hours. A blank experiment is also performed, using the same quantities of chloroform and Hübl reagent, and allowing to stand for the same length of time.

After the expiration of four hours 20 c.c. of 10 per cent. solution of potassium iodide and 150 c.c. water are added to the contents of the bottle, and the excess of iodine titrated with N/10 sodium thiosulphate solution, the whole being well agitated during the titration, which is finished with starch paste as indicator. The blank experiment is titrated in the same manner, and from the amount of thiosulphate required in the blank experiment is deducted the number of c.c. required by the unabsorbed iodine in the other bottle; this figure multiplied by the iodine equivalent of 1 c.c. of the thiosulphate solution and by 100, dividing the product by the weight of fat taken, gives the "Iodine Number".

Example.—1 c.c. of the N/10 sodium thiosulphate solution is found equal to 0.0126 gramme iodine.

0.3187 gramme of fat taken. Blank requires 48.5 c.c. thiosulphate.

Bottle containing oil requires 40.0 c.c. thiosulphate.

48.5 - 40.0 = 8.5, and the iodine absorption of the fat is—

$$\frac{8.5 \times 0.0126 \times 100}{0.3187} = 33.6.$$

Wijs showed that by the employment of a solution of iodine monochloride in glacial acetic acid reliable iodine figures are obtained in a much shorter time, thirty minutes being sufficient, and this method is now in much more general use than the Hübl. Wijs' iodine reagent is made by dissolving 13 grammes iodine in 1 litre of glacial acetic acid and passing chlorine into the solution until the iodine is all converted into iodine monochloride. The process is carried out in exactly the same way as with the Hübl solution except that the fat is preferably dissolved in carbon tetrachloride instead of in chloroform.

Bromine absorption has now been almost entirely superseded by the iodine absorption, although there are several good methods. The gravimetric method of Hehner (*Analyst*, 1895, 49) was employed by one of us for many years with very good results, whilst the bromine-thermal test of Hehner and Mitchell (*Analyst*, 1895, 146) gives rapid and satisfactory results. More recently MacIlhiney (*Jour. Amer. Chem. Soc.*, 1899, 1084-1089) drew attention to bromine absorption methods and tried to rewaken interest in them.

The *Refractive index* is sometimes useful for discriminating between various oils and fats, and, in conjunction with other physical and chemical data, affords another means of detecting adulteration.

Where a great number of samples have to be tested expeditiously, the Abbé refractometer or the Zeiss butyro-refractometer may be recommended on account of the ease with which they are manipulated. The most usual temperature of observations is 60° C.

The *Titre* or setting point of the fatty acids was devised by Dalican, and is generally accepted in the commercial valuation of solid fats as a gauge of firmness, and in the case of tallow has a considerable bearing on the market value.

One ounce of the fat is melted in a shallow porcelain dish, and 30 c.c. of a 25 per cent. caustic soda solution added, together with 50 c.c. of redistilled methylated spirit. The whole is stirred down on the water bath until a pasty soap is obtained, when another 50 c.c. of methylated spirit is added, which redissolves the soap, and the whole again stirred down to a solid soap. This is then dissolved in distilled water, a slight excess of dilute sulphuric acid added to liberate the fatty acids, and the whole warmed until the fatty acids form a clear liquid on the surface. The water beneath the fatty acids is then syphoned off, more distilled water added to wash out any trace of mineral acid remaining, and again syphoned off, this process being repeated until the washings are no longer acid to litmus paper, when the fatty acids are poured on to a dry filter paper, which is inserted in a funnel resting on a beaker, and the latter placed on the water-bath, where it is left until the clear fatty acids have filtered through.

About 10-15 grammes of the pure fatty acids are now transferred to a test tube, 6" × 1", warmed until molten, and the tube introduced through a hole in the cork into a flask or wide-mouthed bottle. A very accurate thermometer, graduated into fifths of a degree Centigrade (previously standardised), is immersed in the fatty acids, so that the bulb is as near the centre as possible, and when the fatty acids just begin to solidify at the bottom of the tube, the thermometer is stirred round slowly. The mercury will descend, and stirring is continued until it ceases to fall further, at which point the thermometer is very carefully observed. It will be found that the temperature will rise rapidly and finally remain stationary for a short time, after which it will again begin to drop until the temperature of the room is reached. The maximum point to which the temperature rises is known as the "titre" of the sample.

ALKALIES AND ALKALI SALTS.

Care should be bestowed upon the sampling of solid caustic soda or potash as the impurities during the solidification always accumulate in the centre of the drum, and an excess of that portion must be avoided or the sample will not be sufficiently representative. The sampling should be performed expeditiously to prevent carbonating, and portions placed in a stoppered bottle. The whole should be slightly broken in a mortar, and bright crystalline portions taken for analysis, using a stoppered weighing bottle.

Caustic Soda and Caustic Potash.—These substances are valued according to the alkali present in the form of caustic (hydrate) and carbonate.

About 2 grammes of the sample are dissolved in 50 c.c. distilled water, and titrated with N/1 sulphuric acid, using phenol-phthalein as indicator, the alkalinity so obtained representing all the caustic alkali and one-half the carbonate, which latter is converted into bicarbonate. One c.c. N/1 acid = 0.031 gramme Na_2O or 0.040 gramme NaOH and 0.047 gramme K_2O, or 0.056 gramme KOH.

After this first titration, the second half of the carbonate may be determined in one of two ways, either:—

(1) By adding from 3-5 c.c. of N/10 acid, and well boiling for five minutes to expel carbonic-acid gas, after which the excess of acid is titrated with N/10 soda solution; or

(2) After adding two drops of methyl orange solution, N/10 acid is run in until the solution acquires a faint pink tint.

In the calculation of the caustic alkali, the number of c.c. of acid required in the second titration, divided by 10, is subtracted from that used in the first, and this difference multiplied by 0.031, or 0.047 gives the amount of Na_2O or K_2O respectively in the weight of sample taken, whence the percentage may be readily calculated.

The proportion of carbonate is calculated by multiplying the amount of N/10 acid required in the second titration by 2, and then by either 0.0031 or 0.0047 to give the amount of carbonate present, expressed as Na_2O or K_2O respectively.

An alternative method is to determine the alkalinity before and after the elimination of carbonate by chloride of barium.

About 7-8 grammes of the sample are dissolved in water, and made up to 100 c.c., and the total alkalinity determined by titrating 20 c.c. with N/1 acid, using methyl orange as indicator. To another 20 c.c. is added barium chloride solution (10 per cent.) until it ceases to give a precipitate, the precipitate allowed to settle, and the clear supernatant liquid decanted off, the precipitate transferred to a filter paper and well washed, and the filtrate titrated with N/1 acid, using phenol-phthalein as indicator. The second titration gives the amount of caustic alkali present, and the difference between the two the proportion of carbonate.

When methyl orange solution is used as indicator, titrations must be carried out cold.

Reference has already been made (p. 39) to the manner in which the alkali percentage is expressed in English degrees in the case of caustic soda.

Chlorides are estimated by titrating the neutral solution with N/10 silver nitrate solution, potassium chromate being used as indicator. One c.c. N/10 $AgNO_3$ solution = 0.00585 gramme sodium chloride.

The amount of acid necessary for exact neutralisation having already been ascertained, it is recommended to use the equivalent quantity of N/10 nitric acid to produce the neutral solution.

Sulphides may be tested for, qualitatively, with lead acetate solution.

Aluminates are determined gravimetrically in the usual manner; 2 grammes are dissolved in water, rendered acid with HCl, excess of ammonia added, and the gelatinous precipitate of aluminium hydrate collected on a filter paper, washed, burnt, and weighed.

Carbonated Alkali (Soda Ash).—The total or available alkali is, of course, the chief factor to be ascertained, and for this purpose it is convenient to weigh out 3.1 grammes of the sample, dissolve in 50 c.c. water, and titrate with N/1 sulphuric or hydrochloric acid, using methyl orange as indicator. Each c.c. of N/1 acid required represents 1 per cent. Na_2O in the sample under examination.

A more complete analysis of soda ash would comprise:—

Insoluble matter, remaining after 10 grammes are dissolved in warm water. This is washed on to a filter-paper, dried, ignited, and weighed.

The filtrate is made up to 200 c.c., and in it may be determined:—

Caustic soda, by titrating with N/1 acid the filtrate resulting from the treatment of 20 c.c. (equal to 1 gramme) with barium chloride solution.

Carbonate.—Titrate 20 c.c. with N/1 acid, and deduct the amount of acid required for the Caustic.

Chlorides.—Twenty c.c. are exactly neutralised with nitric acid, titrated with N/10 $AgNO_3$ solution, using potassium chromate as indicator.

Sulphates.—Twenty c.c. are acidulated with HCl, and the sulphates precipitated with barium chloride; the precipitate is collected on a filter paper, washed, dried, ignited, and weighed, the result being calculated to Na_2SO_4.

Sulphides and Sulphites.—The presence of these compounds is denoted by the evolution of sulphuretted hydrogen and sulphurous acid respectively when the sample is acidulated. Sulphides may also be tested for, qualitatively, with lead acetate solution, or test-paper of sodium nitro-prusside.

The total quantity of these compounds may be ascertained by acidulating with acetic acid, and titrating with N/10 iodine solution, using starch paste as indicator. One c.c. N/10 iodine solution = 0.0063 gramme Na_2SO_3.

The amount of sulphides may be estimated by titrating the hot soda solution, to which ammonia has been added, with an ammoniacal silver nitrate solution, 1 c.c. of which corresponds to 0.005 gramme Na_2S. As the titration proceeds, the precipitate is filtered off, and the addition of ammoniacal silver solution to the filtrate continued until a drop produces only a slight opacity. The presence of chloride, sulphate, hydrate, or carbonate does not interfere with the accuracy of this method. The ammoniacal silver nitrate solution is prepared by dissolving 13.345 grammes of pure silver in pure nitric acid, adding 250 c.c. liquor ammoniæ fortis, and diluting to 1 litre.

Carbonate of Potash (Pearl Ash).—The total or available alkali may be estimated by taking 6.9 grammes of the sample, and titrating with N/1 acid directly, or adding 100 c.c. N/1 sulphuric acid, boiling for a few minutes, and titrating the excess of acid with N/1 caustic soda solution, using litmus as indicator. In this case each c.c. N/1 acid required, is equivalent, in the absence of Na_2CO_3, to 1 per cent. K_2CO_3.

Carbonate of potash may be further examined for the following:—

Moisture.—From 2-3 grammes are heated for thirty minutes in a crucible over a gas flame, and weighed when cold, the loss in weight representing the moisture.

Insoluble residue, remaining after solution in water, filtering and well washing.

Potassium may be determined by precipitation as potassium platino-chloride thus:—Dissolve 0.5 gramme in a small quantity (say 10 c.c.) of water, and carefully acidulate with hydrochloric acid, evaporate the resultant liquor to dryness in a tared platinum basin, and heat the residue gradually to dull redness. Cool in a desicator, weigh, and express the result as "mixed chlorides," *i.e.* chlorides of soda and potash. To the mixed chlorides add 10 c.c. water, and platinic chloride in excess (the quantity may be three times the amount of the mixed chlorides) and evaporate nearly to dryness; add 15 c.c. alcohol and allow to stand three hours covered with a watch-glass, giving the dish a gentle rotatory movement occasionally. The clear liquid is decanted through a tared filter, and the precipitate well washed with alcohol by decantation, and finally transferred to the filter, dried and weighed. From the weight of potassium platino-chloride, K_2PtCl_6, is calculated the amount of potassium oxide K_2O by the use of the factor 94/488.2 or 0.19254.

Chlorides, determined with N/10 silver nitrate solution, and calculated to KCl.

Sulphates, estimated as barium sulphate, and calculated to K_2SO_4.

Sodium Carbonate, found by deducting the K_2CO_3 corresponding to the actual potassium as determined above, from the total alkali.

Iron, precipitated with excess of ammonia, filtered, ignited, and weighed as Fe_2O_3.

SODIUM CHLORIDE (COMMON SALT).

This should be examined for the following:—

Actual Chloride, either titrated with N/10 silver nitrate solution, using neutral potassium chromate solution as indicator, or, preferably, estimated gravimetrically as silver chloride by precipitation with silver nitrate solution, the precipitate transferred to a tared filter paper, washed, dried and weighed.

Insoluble matter, remaining on dissolving 5 grammes in water, and filtering. This is washed, dried, ignited and weighed.

Moisture.—5 grammes are weighed into a platinum crucible, and heat gently applied. The temperature is gradually increased to a dull red heat, which is maintained for a few minutes, the dish cooled in a desicator, and weighed.

Sulphates are estimated by precipitation as barium sulphate and calculated to Na_2SO_4.

Sodium.—This may be determined by converting the salt into sodium sulphate by the action of concentrated sulphuric acid, igniting to drive off hydrochloric and sulphuric acids, and fusing the mass until constant in weight, weighing finally as Na_2SO_4.

POTASSIUM CHLORIDE.

This should be examined, in the same way as sodium chloride, for chloride, insoluble matter, moisture, and sulphate. The potassium may be determined as potassium platino-chloride, as described under carbonate of potash.

SILICATES OF SODA AND POTASH.

The most important determinations for these are total alkali and silica.

Total alkali is estimated by dissolving 2 grammes in distilled water, and titrating when cold, with N/1 acid, using methyl orange as indicator.

Silica may be determined by dissolving 1 gramme in distilled water, rendering the solution acid with HCl, and evaporating to complete dryness on the water-bath, after which the residue is moistened with HCl and again evaporated, this operation being repeated a third time. The residue is then heated to about 150° C., extracted with hot dilute HCl, filtered, thoroughly washed, dried, ignited in a tared platinum crucible, and weighed as SiO_2.

ESSENTIAL OILS.

As already stated, these are very liable to adulteration, and an examination of all kinds of oil is desirable, while in the case of the more expensive varieties it should never be omitted.

Specific Gravity.—As with fats and oils, this is usually taken at 15° C., and compared with water at the same temperature. In the case of otto of rose and guaiac wood oil, however, which are solid at this temperature, it is generally observed at 30° C. compared with water at 15° C.

The specific gravity is preferably taken in a bottle or U-tube, but if sufficient of the oil is available and a high degree of accuracy is not necessary, it may be taken either with a Westphal balance, or by means of a hydrometer.

Optical Rotation.—For this purpose a special instrument, known as a polarimeter, is required, details of the construction and use of which would be out of place here. Suffice it to mention that temperature plays an important part in the determination of the optical activity of certain essential oils, notably in the case of lemon and orange oils. For these Gildemeister and Hoffmann give the following corrections:—

Lemon oil, below 20° C. subtract 9' for each degree below, above 20° C. add 8' for each degree above.

Orange oil, below 20° C. subtract 14' for each degree below, above 20° C. add 13' for each degree above.

Refractive Index.—This figure is occasionally useful, and is best determined with an Abbé refractometer, at 20° C.

Solubility in Alcohol.—This is found by running alcohol of the requisite strength from a burette into a measured volume of the oil with constant agitation, until the oil forms a clear solution with the alcohol. Having noted the quantity of alcohol added, it is well to run in a small further quantity of alcohol, and observe whether any opalescence or cloudiness appears.

Acid, *ester*, and *saponification values* are determined exactly as described under fats and oils. Instead of expressing the result as saponification value or number, the percentage of ester, calculated in the form of the most important ester present, may be obtained by multiplying the number of c.c. of N/1 alkali absorbed in the saponification by the molecular weight of the ester. Thus, to find the percentage as linalyl acetate, the number of c.c. absorbed would be multiplied by 0.196 and by 100, and divided by the weight of oil taken.

Alcohols.—For the estimation of these, if the oil contains much ester it must first be saponified with alcoholic potash, to liberate the combined alcohols, and after neutralising the excess of alkali with acid, the oil is washed into a separating funnel with water, separated, dried with anhydrous sodium sulphate, and is then ready for the alcohol determination.

If there is only a small quantity of ester present, this preliminary saponification is unnecessary.

The alcohols are estimated by conversion into their acetic esters, which are then saponified with standard alcoholic potash, thereby furnishing a measure of the amount of alcohol esterified.

Ten c.c. of the oil is placed in a flask with an equal volume of acetic anhydride, and 2 grammes of anhydrous sodium acetate, and gently boiled for an hour to an hour and a half. After cooling, water is added, and the contents of the flask heated on the water-bath for fifteen to thirty minutes, after which they are cooled, transferred to a separating funnel, and washed with a brine solution until the washings cease to give an acid reaction with litmus paper. The oil is now dried with anhydrous sodium sulphate, filtered, and 1-2 grammes weighed into a flask and saponified with alcoholic potash as in the determination of ester or saponification value.

The calculation is a little complicated, but an example may perhaps serve to make it clear.

A geranium oil containing 26.9 per cent. of ester, calculated as geranyl tiglate, was acetylated, after saponification, to liberate the combined geraniol, and 2.3825 grammes of the acetylated oil required 9.1 c.c. of N/1 alkali for its saponification.

Now every 196 grammes of geranyl acetate present in the acetylated oil correspond to 154 grammes of geraniol, so that for every 196 grammes of ester now present in the oil, 42 grammes have been added to its weight, and it is therefore necessary to make a deduction from the weight of oil taken for the final saponification to allow for this, and since each c.c. of N/1 alkali absorbed corresponds to 0.196 gramme of geranyl acetate, the amount to be deducted is found by multiplying the number of c.c. absorbed by 0.042 gramme, the formula for the estimation of total alcohols thus becoming in the example given:—

$$\text{Per cent. of geraniol} = \frac{9.1 \times 0.154 \times 100}{2.3825 - (9.1 \times 0.042)} = 70.2$$

The percentage of combined alcohols can be calculated from the amount of ester found, and by subtracting this from the percentage of total alcohols, that of the free alcohols is obtained.

In the example quoted, the ester corresponds to 17.6 per cent. geraniol, and this, deducted from the total alcohols, gives 52.6 per cent. free alcohols, calculated as geraniol.

This process gives accurate results with geraniol, borneol, and menthol, but with linalol and terpineol the figures obtained are only comparative, a considerable quantity of these alcohols being decomposed during the acetylation.

The aldehyde citronellal is converted by acetic anhydride into isopulegol acetate, so that this is also included in the determination of graniol in citronella oil.

Phenols.—These bodies are soluble in alkalies, and may be estimated by measuring 5 c.c. or 10 c.c. of the oil into a Hirschsohn flask (a flask of about 100 c.c. capacity with a long narrow neck holding 10 c.c., graduated in tenths of a c.c.), adding 25 c.c. of a 5 per cent. aqueous caustic potash solution, and warming in the water-bath, then adding another 25 c.c., and after one hour in the water-bath filling the flask with the potash solution until the unabsorbed oil rises into the neck of the flask, the volume of this oil being read off when it has cooled down to the temperature of the laboratory. From the volume of oil dissolved the percentage of phenols is readily calculated.

Aldehydes.—In the estimation of these substances, use is made of their property of combining with sodium bisulphite to form compounds soluble in hot water. From 5-10 c.c. of the oil is measured into a Hirschsohn flask, about 30 c.c. of a hot saturated solution of sodium bisulphite added, and the flask immersed in a boiling water bath, and thoroughly shaken at frequent intervals. Further quantities of the bisulphite solution are gradually added, until, after about one hour, the unabsorbed oil rises into the neck of the flask, where, after cooling, its volume is read off, and the percentage of absorbed oil, or aldehydes, calculated.

In the case of lemon oil, where the proportion of aldehydes, though of great importance, is relatively very small, it is necessary to first concentrate the aldehydes before determining them. For this purpose, 100 c.c. of the oil is placed in a Ladenburg fractional distillation flask, and 90 c.c. distilled off under a pressure of not more than 40 mm., and the residue steam distilled. The oil so obtained is separated from the condensed water, measured, dried, and 5 c.c. assayed for aldehydes either by the process already described, or by the following process devised by Burgess (*Analyst*, 1904, 78):—

Five c.c. of the oil are placed in the Hirschsohn flask, about 20 c.c. of a saturated solution of neutral sodium sulphite added, together with a few drops of rosolic acid solution as indicator, and the flask placed in a boiling water-bath and continually agitated. The contents of the flask soon become red owing to the liberation of free alkali by the combination of the aldehyde with part of the sodium sulphite, and this coloration is just discharged by the addition of sufficient 10 per cent. acetic-acid solution. The flask is again placed in the water-bath, the shaking continued, and any further alkali liberated neutralised by more acetic acid, the process being continued in this way until no further red colour is produced. The flask is then filled with the sodium sulphite solution, the volume of the cooled unabsorbed oil read off, and the percentage of aldehydes calculated as before.

Solidifying Point, or Congealing Point.—This is of some importance in the examination of anise and fennel oils, and is also useful in the examination of otto of rose. A suitable apparatus may be made by obtaining three test tubes, of different sizes, which will fit one inside the other, and fixing them together in this way through corks. The innermost tube is then filled with the oil, and a sensitive thermometer, similar to that described under the Titre test for fats, suspended with its bulb completely immersed in the oil. With anise and fennel, the oil is cooled down with constant stirring until it just starts crystallising, when the stirring is interrupted, and the maximum temperature to which the mercury rises noted. This is the solidifying point.

In the case of otto of rose, the otto is continually stirred, and the point at which the first crystal is observed is usually regarded as the congealing point.

Melting Point.—This is best determined by melting some of the solid oil, or crystals, and sucking a small quantity up into a capillary tube, which is then attached by a rubber band to the bulb of the thermometer, immersed in a suitable bath (water, glycerine, oil, etc.) and the temperature of the bath gradually raised until the substance in the tube is sufficiently melted to rise to the surface, the temperature at which this takes place being the melting point.

The melting point of otto of rose is usually taken in a similar tube to the setting point, and is considered to be the point at which the last crystal disappears.

Iodine Absorption.—In the authors' opinion, this is of some value in conjunction with other data in judging of the purity of otto of rose. It is determined by Hübl's process as described under Fats and Oils, except that only 0.1 to 0.2 gramme is taken, and instead of 10 c.c. of chloroform, 10 c.c. of pure alcohol are added. The rest of the process is identical.

SOAP.

In the analysis of soap, it is a matter of considerable importance that all the determinations should be made on a uniform and average sample of the soap, otherwise very misleading and unreliable figures are obtained. Soap very rapidly loses its moisture on the surface, while the interior of the bar or cake may be comparatively moist, and the best way is to carefully remove the outer edges and take the portions for analysis from the centre. In the case of a household or unmilled toilet soap, it is imperative that the quantities for analysis should all be weighed out as quickly after each other as possible.

Fatty Acids.—Five grammes of the soap are rapidly weighed into a small beaker, distilled water added, and the beaker heated on the water bath until the soap is dissolved.

A slight excess of mineral acid is now added, and the whole heated until the separated fatty acids are perfectly clear, when they are collected on a tared filter paper, well washed with hot water and dried until constant in weight. The result multiplied by 20 gives the percentage of fatty acids in the sample.

A quicker method, and one which gives accurate results when care is bestowed upon it, is to proceed in the manner described above as far as the decomposition with mineral acid, and to then add 5 or 10 grammes of stearic acid or beeswax to the contents of the beaker and heat until a clear layer of fatty matter collects upon the acid liquor.

Cool the beaker, and when the cake is sufficiently hard, remove it carefully by means of a spatula and dry on a filtering paper, add the portions adhering to the sides of the beaker to the cake, and weigh.

The weight, less the amount of stearic acid or beeswax added, multiplied by 20 gives the percentage of fatty acids.

Care must be taken that the cake does not contain enclosed water.

The results of these methods are returned as fatty acids, but are in reality insoluble fatty acids, the soluble fatty acids being generally disregarded. However in soaps made from cocoa-nut and palm-kernel oils (which contain an appreciable quantity of soluble fatty acids) the acid liquor is shaken with ether, and, after evaporation of the ethereal extract, the amount of fatty matter left is added to the result already obtained as above, or the ether method described below may be advantageously employed.

Where the soap under examination contains mineral matter, the separated fatty acids may be dissolved in ether. This is best performed in an elongated, graduated, stoppered tube, the total volume of the ether, after subsidence, carefully read, and an aliquot part taken and evaporated to dryness in a tared flask, which is placed in the oven at 100° C. until the weight is constant.

In a complete analysis, the figure for fatty acids should be converted into terms of fatty anhydrides by multiplying by the factor 0.9875.

In this test the resin acids contained in the soap are returned as fatty acids, but the former can be estimated, as described later, and deducted from the total.

Total Alkali.—The best method is to incinerate 5 grammes of the soap in a platinum dish, dissolve the residue in water, boil and filter, making the volume of filtrate up to 250 c.c., the solution being reserved for the subsequent determination of salt, silicates, and sulphates, as detailed below.

Fifty c.c. of the solution are titrated with N/1 acid, to methyl orange, and the result expressed in terms of Na_2O.

Number of c.c. required × 0.031 × 100 = per cent. Na_2O.

The total alkali may also be estimated in the filtrate from the determination of fatty acids, if the acid used for decomposing the soap solution has been measured and its strength known, by titrating back the excess of acid with normal soda solution, when the difference will equal the amount of total alkali in the quantity taken.

The total alkali is usually expressed in the case of hard soaps as Na_2O, and in soft soaps as K_2O.

Free caustic alkali is estimated by dissolving 2 grammes of the soap, in neutral pure alcohol, with gentle heat, filtering, well washing the filter with hot neutral spirit, and titrating the filtrate with N/10 acid, to phenol-phthalein.

Number of c.c. required × 0.0031 × 50 = per cent. free alkali Na_2O, as caustic.

Free Carbonated Alkali.—The residue on the filter paper from the above determination is washed with hot water, and the aqueous filtrate titrated with N/10 acid, using methyl orange as indicator. The result is generally expressed in terms of Na_2O.

Number of c.c. required × 0.0031 × 50 = per cent. free alkali Na_2O, as carbonate.

Free Alkali.—Some analysts determine the alkalinity to phenol-phthalein of the alcoholic soap solution without filtering, and express it as free alkali (caustic, carbonates, or any salt having an alkaline reaction).

Combined Alkali.—The difference between total alkali and free alkali (caustic and carbonate together) represents the alkali combined with fatty acids. This figure may also be directly determined by titrating, with N/2 acid, the alcoholic solution of soap after the free caustic estimation, using lacmoid as indicator.

The potash and soda in soaps may be separated by the method described for the estimation of potassium in *Pearl ash* (page 126).

The potassium platino-chloride (K_2PtCl_6) is calculated to potassium chloride (KCl) by using the factor 0.3052, and this figure deducted from the amount of mixed chlorides found, gives the amount of sodium chloride (NaCl), from which the sodium oxide (Na_2O) is obtained by multiplying by 0.52991.

The potassium chloride (KCl) is converted into terms of potassium oxide (K_2O) by the use of the factor 0.63087.

Salt may be determined in 50 c.c. of the filtered aqueous extract of the incinerated soap, by exactly neutralising with normal acid and titrating with N/10 silver nitrate solution, using a neutral solution of potassium chromate as indicator. The final reaction is more distinctly observed if a little bicarbonate of soda is added to the solution.

Number of c.c. required × 0.00585 × 100 = per cent. of common salt, NaCl.

Chlorides may also be estimated by Volhard's method, the aqueous extract being rendered slightly acid with nitric acid, a measured volume of N/10 silver nitrate solution added, and the excess titrated back with N/10 ammonium thiocyanate solution, using iron alum as indicator.

Silicates.—These are estimated by evaporating 50 c.c. of the filtered extract from the incinerated soap, in a platinum dish with hydrochloric acid twice to complete dryness, heating to 150° C., adding hot water, and filtering through a tared filter paper.

The residue is well washed, ignited, and weighed as SiO_2, and from this silica is calculated the sodium silicate.

Sulphates may be determined in the filtrate from the silica estimation by precipitation with barium chloride solution, and weighing the barium sulphate, after filtering, and burning, expressing the result in terms of Na_2SO_4 by the use of the factor 0.6094.

Moisture.—This is simply estimated by taking a weighed portion in small shavings in a tared dish, and drying in the oven at 105° C. until it ceases to lose weight. From the loss thus found is calculated the moisture percentage.

Free or Uncombined Fat.—This is usually determined by repeated extraction of an aqueous solution of the soap with petroleum ether; the ethereal solution, after washing with water to remove traces of soap, is evaporated to dryness and the residue weighed.

A good method, which can be recommended for employment where many determinations have to be performed, is to dissolve 10 grammes of soap in 50 c.c. neutral alcohol and titrate to phenol-phthalein with N/1 acid. Add 3-5 drops HCl and boil to expel carbonic acid, neutralise with alcoholic KOH solution and add exactly 10 c.c. in excess, boil for fifteen minutes under a reflux condenser and titrate with N/1 acid. The difference between this latter figure and the amount required for a blank test with 10 c.c. alcoholic KOH, denotes the amount of alkali absorbed by the uncombined fat.

Examination of the fatty acids as a guide to the probable composition of the soap:—

From the data obtained by estimating the "titre," iodine number, and saponification equivalent of the mixed fatty and rosin acids, and the rosin content, a fairly good idea of the constitution of the soap may be deduced.

The titre, iodine number, and saponification equivalent are determined in exactly the same manner as described under Fats and Oils.

The presence of rosin may be detected by the Liebermann-Storch reaction, which consists in dissolving a small quantity of the fatty acids in acetic anhydride, and adding to a few drops of this solution 1 drop of 50 per cent. sulphuric acid. A violet coloration is produced with rosin acids. The amount of rosin may be estimated by the method devised by Twitchell (*Journ. Soc. Chem. Ind.*, 1891, 804) which is carried out thus:—

Two grammes of the mixed fatty and rosin acids are dissolved in 20 c.c. absolute alcohol, and dry hydrochloric acid gas passed through until no more is absorbed, the flask being kept cool by means of cold water to prevent the rosin acids being acted upon. The flask, after disconnecting, is allowed to stand one hour to ensure complete combination, when its contents are transferred to a Philips' beaker, well washed out with water so that the volume is increased about five times, and boiled until the acid solution is clear, a fragment of granulated zinc being added to prevent bumping. The heat is removed, and the liquid allowed to cool, when it is poured into a separator, and the beaker thoroughly rinsed out with ether. After shaking, the acid liquor is withdrawn, and the ethereal layer washed with water until free from acid. Fifty c.c. neutral alcohol are added, and the solution titrated with N/1 KOH or NaOH solution, the percentage of rosin being calculated from its combining weight. Twitchell suggests 346 as the combining weight of rosin, but 330 is a closer approximation.

The method may be also carried out gravimetrically, in which case petroleum ether, boiling at 74° C. is used for washing out the beaker into the separator. The acid liquor is run off, and the petroleum ether layer washed first with water and then with a solution of 1/2 gramme KOH and 5 c.c. alcohol in 50 c.c. water, and agitated. The rosin is thus saponified and separated. The resinate solution is withdrawn, acidified, and the resin acids collected, dried and weighed.

Halphen's Reaction.—This is a special test to determine the presence or absence of cotton-seed oil fatty acids in mixtures. Equal parts of the fatty acids, amyl alcohol, and a 1 per cent. solution of sulphur in carbon bisulphide, are heated in a test-tube placed in a water-bath until effervescence ceases, then in boiling brine for one hour or longer when only small quantities are present. The presence of cotton-seed oil is denoted by a pink coloration. The reaction is rendered much more rapid, according to Rupp (*Z. Untersuch. Nahr. Genussm.*, 1907, 13, 74), by heating in a stoppered flask.

Other bodies which it is occasionally necessary to test for or determine in soap include:—

Carbolic acid.—Fifty grammes of the soap are dissolved in water and 20 c.c. of 10 per cent. caustic potash added. The solution is treated with an excess of brine, the supernatant liquor separated, and the precipitate washed with brine, the washings being added to the liquor withdrawn. This is then evaporated to a small bulk, placed in a Muter's graduated tube, and acidified with mineral acid.

The volume of separated phenols is observed and stated in percentage on the soap taken.

Or the alkaline layer may be rendered acid and steam distilled; the distillate is made up to a known volume, and a portion titrated by the Koppeschaar method with standard bromine water.

Glycerine.—Five grammes of soap are dissolved in water, decomposed with dilute sulphuric acid, and the clear fatty acids filtered and washed. The filtrate is neutralised with barium carbonate, evaporated to 50 c.c., and the glycerol estimated by the bichromate method detailed under Crude Glycerine.

Starch or *gum* may be detected by dissolving the soap in alcohol, filtering, and examining the residue on the filter paper. Starch is readily recognised by the blue coloration it gives with a solution of iodine in potassium iodide.

Sugars are tested for by means of Fehlings' solution, in the liquor separated from the fatty acids, after first boiling with dilute acid to invert any cane sugar.

Mercury will be revealed by a black precipitate produced when sulphuretted hydrogen is added to the liquor separated from the fatty acids, and may be estimated by filtering off this precipitate on a tared Gooch's crucible, which is then dried and weighed.

Borax or borates are tested for in the residue insoluble in alcohol. This is dissolved in water, rendered faintly acid with dilute hydrochloric acid, and a strip of turmeric paper immersed for a few minutes in the liquid. This is then dried in the water-oven, when if any boric acid compound is present, a bright reddish-pink stain is produced on the paper, which is turned blue on moistening with dilute alkali.

The amount of the boric acid radicle may be determined by incinerating 5-10 grammes of soap, extracting with hot dilute acid, filtering, neutralising this solution to methyl orange, and boiling to expel carbon dioxide. After cooling, sufficient pure neutralised glycerine is added to form one-third of the total volume, and the liquid titrated with N/2 caustic soda solution, using phenol-phthalein as indicator. Each c.c. of N/2 NaOH solution corresponds to 0.031 gramme crystallised boric acid, H_3BO_3 or 0.0477 gramme crystallised borax, $Na_2B_4O_7 \cdot 10H_2O$.

LYES.

The amounts of caustic alkali (if any), carbonated alkali, and salt present are determined in the manner already described under Alkali and Alkali Salts. The glycerol content is ascertained by taking 2.5 grammes, adding lead subacetate solution, and filtering without increasing the bulk more than is absolutely necessary; the solution is concentrated to about 25 c.c., and the oxidation with bichromate and sulphuric acid conducted as described in the examination of Crude Glycerine. The solution, after oxidation, is made up to 250 c.c., and titrated against standard ferrous ammonium sulphate solution, the formula for the calculation being:—

$$\text{Per cent. of glycerol} = (0.25 - (2.5/n)) \times 40$$

where n equals the number of c.c. of oxidised lyes required to oxidise the ferrous ammonium sulphate solution.

The estimation of actual glycerol in this is necessarily a matter of considerable importance, and a very large number of processes, which are constantly being added to, have been suggested for the purpose. Hitherto, however, only two methods have been generally adopted, *viz.* the acetin and the bichromate processes. Unfortunately the results obtained by these do not invariably agree, the latter, which includes all oxidisable matter as glycerol, giving sometimes considerably higher results, and it has been suggested that a determination should be made by both methods, and the average of the two results considered the true value. This involves a considerable amount of time and trouble, and it will generally be found sufficient in a works laboratory to determine the glycerol by one method only in the ordinary course, reserving the other process for use as a check in case of dispute or doubt.

Acetin Method.—This consists in converting the glycerol into its ester with acetic acid, the acetic triglyceride, or triacetin being formed. This is then saponified with a known volume of standard alkali, the excess of which is titrated with acid, and the percentage of glycerol calculated from the amount of alkali absorbed.

From 1 to 1.5 grammes of the glycerine is weighed into a conical flask of about 150 c.c. capacity, 7 or 8 c.c. of acetic anhydride added, together with about 3 grammes of anhydrous sodium acetate, and the whole boiled on a sand-bath under a reflux condenser for one to one and a half hours, after which it is allowed to cool, 50 c.c. water added, and the ester dissolved by shaking, and gently warming, the reflux condenser still being attached as the acetin is very volatile. The solution is then filtered from a white flocculent precipitate, which contains most of the impurities, into a larger conical flask, of some 500-600 c.c. capacity, and after cooling, rendered just neutral to phenolphthalein by means of N/2 caustic soda solution, the exact point being reached when the solution acquires a reddish-yellow tint; 25 c.c. of a strong caustic soda solution is then added, and the liquid boiled for about fifteen minutes, the excess of alkali being titrated after cooling, with N/1 or N/2 hydrochloric acid. A blank experiment is carried out simultaneously, with another 25 c.c. of the soda solution, and the difference in the amounts of acid required by the two, furnishes a measure of the alkali required to saponify the acetin formed, and hence the amount of glycerol in the crude glycerine may be calculated.

Example.—1.4367 grammes crude glycerine, after treatment with acetic anhydride, and neutralising, was saponified with 25 c.c. of a 10 per cent. caustic soda solution.

The blank experiment	required	111.05 c.c.	N/1	hydrochloric acid.
Flask containing acetin	"	75.3 c.c.	"	"

$$35.75 \text{ c.c.} \quad " \quad "$$

Hence, the acetin formed from the glycerol present in 1.4367 grammes of the crude glycerine required 35.75 c.c. N/1 caustic alkali for its saponification, so that the percentage of glycerol may be calculated from the following formula:—

$$\text{Per cent. glycerol} = \frac{35.75 \times 0.03067 \times 100}{1.4367} = 76.3.$$

Bichromate Method.—This process was originally devised by Hehner (*Journ. Soc. Chem. Ind.*, 1889, 4-9), but the modification suggested by Richardson and Jaffe (*ibid.*, 1898, 330) is preferred by the authors, and has been practised by them for several years with perfectly satisfactory results.

Twenty-five grammes of the crude glycerine are weighed out in a beaker, washed into a 250 c.c. stoppered flask, and made up to the graduation mark with water. Twenty-five c.c. of this solution are then measured from a burette into a small beaker, a slight excess of basic lead acetate solution added to precipitate organic matter, the precipitate allowed to settle, and the supernatant liquid poured through a filter paper into another 250 c.c. flask. The precipitate is washed by decantation until the flask is nearly full, then transferred to the filter, and allowed to drain, a few drops of dilute sulphuric acid being added to precipitate the slight excess of basic lead acetate solution, and the contents of the flask made up with water to 250 c.c. This solution is filtered, 20 c.c. measured from a burette into a conical flask of about

150 c.c. capacity, 25 c.c. of a standard potassium bichromate solution containing 74.86 grammes bichromate per litre added, together with 50 c.c. of 50 per cent. sulphuric acid, and the whole placed in a boiling water-bath for one hour, after which it is allowed to cool, diluted with water to 250 c.c., and this solution run in to 20 c.c. of a 3 per cent. ferrous ammonium sulphate solution until the latter is completely oxidised, as shown by no blue coloration being produced when one drop is brought into contact with one drop of a freshly prepared solution of potassium ferricyanide on a spot-plate. The ferrous ammonium sulphate solution is previously standardised by titration with a potassium bichromate solution of one-tenth the above strength, made by diluting 10 c.c. of the strong solution to 100 c.c. with water.

The reaction taking place in the oxidation may be represented by the equation:—

$3C_3H_5(OH)_3 + 7K_2Cr_2O_7 + 28H_2SO_4 = 9CO_2 + 40H_2O + 7K_2SO_4 + 7Cr_2(SO_4)_3$.

Now the strong potassium bichromate solution above mentioned is of such a strength that 1 c.c. will oxidise 0.01 gramme glycerine, and 20 c.c. of the ferrous ammonium sulphate solution should require about 10 c.c. of the one-tenth strength bichromate in the blank experiment. If it requires more or less than this, then the amount of ferrous ammonium sulphate solution which would require exactly 10 c.c. (corresponding to 0.01 gramme glycerine) is calculated, and the oxidised glycerine solution run into this until oxidation is complete.

The formula for the calculation of the percentage of glycerol then becomes:—

Per cent. of glycerol = $(0.25 - ((250 \times 0.01)/n)) \times 500$, where n equals the number of c.c. of oxidised glycerine solution required to oxidise the ferrous ammonium sulphate solution.

Example:—

In the blank experiment 20 c.c. ferrous ammonium sulphate solution required 9.8 c.c. one-tenth strength bichromate solution, so that 20.4 c.c. ferrous solution would equal 10 c.c. bichromate.

20.4 c.c. ferrous solution required 27.8 c.c. of oxidised glycerine solution before it ceased to give a blue coloration with potassium ferricyanide.

Therefore, per cent. of glycerol = $(0.25 - ((250 \times 0.01)/27.8)) \times 500$,

= 80.04 per cent.

Other methods have been suggested for the preliminary purification, *e.g.*, silver oxide, silver carbonate and lead subacetate, and copper sulphate and caustic potash, but the lead subacetate alone with care gives satisfactory results.

Other determinations include those of specific gravity, alkalinity, proportion of salts and chloride, and tests for metals, arsenic, sulphur compounds, sugar, and fatty acids.

Specific gravity is determined at 15° C., and may be taken in specific gravity bottle, or with a Westphal balance or hydrometer It usually ranges from 1.3 to 1.31.

Alkalinity, which is usually sodium carbonate, and may be somewhat considerable if the soap has been grained with caustic alkali, is determined after dilution with water by titrating with N/2 acid, using methyl orange as indicator.

Salts.—These may be determined by gently incinerating 5-6 grammes of the glycerine, extracting the carbonaceous mass with distilled water, filtering, and evaporating the filtrate on the water bath. The dried residue represents the salts in the weight taken.

Chloride of sodium (common salt) may be estimated by dissolving the total salts in water, adding potassium chromate, and titrating with N/10 silver nitrate solution.

Copper, *lead*, *iron*, *magnesium*, and *calcium* may also be tested for in the salts, by ordinary reactions.

Arsenic is best tested for by the Gutzeit method. About 5 c.c. is placed in a test-tube, a few fragments of granulated zinc free from arsenic, and 10 c.c. dilute hydrochloric acid added, and the mouth of the tube covered with a small filter paper, moistened three successive times with an alcoholic solution of mercury bichloride and dried. After thirty minutes the filter paper is examined, when a yellow stain will be observed if arsenic is present.

Sulphates.—These may be precipitated with barium chloride in acid solution, in the usual way, dried, ignited, and weighed.

Sulphites give with barium chloride a precipitate soluble in hydrochloric acid. If the precipitate is well washed with hot water, and a few drops of iodine solution together with starch paste added, the presence of sulphites is proved by the gradual disappearance of the blue starch-iodine compound first formed.

Thiosulphates are detected by precipitating any sulphite and sulphate with barium chloride, filtering, acidifying, and adding a few drops of potassium permanganate solution, when in the presence of a mere trace of thiosulphate, the solution becomes cloudy.

Sulphides.—Lewkowitsch recommends testing for these by replacing the mercury bichloride with lead acetate paper in the Gutzeit arsenic test. Any sulphide causes a blackening of the lead acetate paper.

Sugars may be tested for both before and after inversion, by boiling with Fehlings' solution, when no reduction should take place, if pure.

Fatty acids are detected by the turbidity they produce when the diluted glycerine is acidified.

CHAPTER XI.

STATISTICS OF THE SOAP INDUSTRY.

Until the year 1853 the amount of soap produced annually in this country was readily obtainable from the official returns collected for the purpose of levying the duty, and the following figures, taken at intervals of ten years for the half century prior to that date, show the steady development of the industry during that period:—

Year.	Manufactured.	Consumed.	Exported.	Duty per Ton.
	Cwts.	Cwts.	Cwts.	£
1801	509,980	482,140	26,790	21
1811	678,570	651,780	26,790	21
1821	875,000	839,290	35,710	28
1831	1,098,210	955,360	142,850	28
1841	1,776,790	1,517,860	258,930	14
1851	1,937,500	1,741,070	196,430	14

Since the repeal of the soap duty, the revenue from which had reached about £1,000,000 per annum, no accurate means of gauging the production exists, but it is estimated that it has nearly quadrupled during the last fifty-five years, being now some 7,000,000 or 8,000,000 cwt. per annum.

The number of soap manufacturers in the United Kingdom is nearly 300, and the amount of capital invested in the industry is roughly estimated to approach £20,000,000 sterling.

Official figures are still available for the amount and value of soap annually imported and exported to and from the United Kingdom, the returns for the last eight years being:—

Imports.

Year.	Household.		Toilet.		Total	
	Quantity.	Value.	Quantity.	Value.	Quantity.	Value
	Cwts.	£	Cwts.	£	Cwts.	£
1900	...	...	...	...	191,233	244,345
1901	...	...	...	...	302,555	315,026
1902	...	...	...	...	361,851	429,300
1903	273,542	284,376	25,749	98,032	462,959	499,407
1904	254,425	268,408	17,962	81,162	383,122	438,966
1905	274,238	279,044	19,631	98,507	473,067	500,430
1906	309,975	311,114	18,554	101,243	399,070	468,086
1907	228,035	263,965	18,244	99,432	504,710	545,385

Household and toilet soaps were not given separately prior to 1903.

The imports during the last three years for which complete figures are obtainable, came from the following sources:—

Household Soap.

	1904.	1905.	1906.
	£	£	£
From Netherlands	4,315	3,620	3,368
France	14,339	17,783	24,747
Italy	24,209	18,129	32,972
United States	218,740	235,612	242,294
Other Foreign Countries	6,785	3,873	7,448
Total from Foreign Countries	268,388	279,017	310,829
Total from British Possessions	20	27	285
Total	268,408	279,044	311,114

Toilet Soap.

	1904.	1905.	1906.
	£	£	£
From Germany	3,509	3,516	3,001
Netherlands	5,937	5,773	5,919
Belgium	1,568	1,861	3,145
France	7,120	7,633	5,794
Italy	1,176	255	1,233
United States	59,863	74,516	78,382
Other Foreign Countries	166	147	196
Total from Foreign Countries	79,339	93,701	97,670

Total from British Possessions	1,823	4,411	3,225
Total		81,162	98,112	100,895

Exports.

The exports from the United Kingdom during the past eight years have been as follows:—

	Household.		Toilet.		Total	
Year.	Quantity.	Value.	Quantity.	Value.	Quantity.	Value.
	Cwts.	£	Cwts.	£	Cwts.	£
1900	...	...	...	...	874,214	939,510
1901	...	...	...	...	947,485	999,524
1902	...	...	...	...	1,051,624	1,126,657
1903	998,995	900,814	38,372	217,928	1,057,164	1,143,661
1904	1,049,022	955,774	40,406	228,574	1,108,174	1,208,712
1905	1,167,976	1,013,837	43,837	248,425	1,230,310	1,284,727
1906	1,131,294	1,009,653	46,364	261,186	1,210,598	1,309,556
1907	1,114,624	1,095,170	50,655	280,186	1,240,805	1,459,113

Household and toilet soaps were not given separately prior to 1903.

The exports for the last three years for which complete figures are available, consisted of the following:—

Household Soap.

	1904.	1905.	1906.
	£	£	£
To Sweden	3,027	2,911	3,677
Norway	4,173	3,921	6,005
Netherlands	39,420	41,197	48,601
Dutch Possessions in the Indian Seas	8,586	10,293	7,746
Belgium	73,996	51,583	7,729
France	11,741	12,222	22,907
Portuguese East Africa	28,987	42,981	40,478
Canary Islands	24,763	27,864	27,579
Italy	2,842	3,187	3,962
Turkey	6,974	7,858	5,897
Egypt	12,110	9,467	12,035
China (exclusive of Hong-Kong and Macao)	49,235	114,156	89,169
United States	3,885	1,975	3,924
Columbia	3,601	501	1,364
Ecuador	3,075	3,096	6,861
Chili	5,972	4,865	9,203
Brazil	35,197	28,198	31,726
Argentine Republic	7,802	8,954	13,084
Other Foreign Countries	40,058	53,914	77,687

Total to Foreign Countries	365,444	429,143	419,634
To Channel Islands	5,301	8,328	7,968
Gibraltar	13,272	13,868	12,661
British West Africa—			
Gold Coast	22,598	18,513	23,423
Lagos	7,751	8,032	9,518
Nigerian Protectorate	14,942	15,299	20,951
Cape of Good Hope	158,517	143,750	136,388
Natal	74,848	71,874	46,771
British India—			
Bombay (including Kurachi)	59,406	68,945	77,867
Madras	6,364	6,697	10,355
Bengal, Eastern Bengal and Assam.	26,534	23,087	22,648
Burmah	26,389	35,727	37,103
Straits Settlements and Dependencies	26,516	32,214	39,749
Hong-Kong	14,119	15,153	15,685
British West India Islands	74,069	58,881	67,331
British Guiana	12,661	12,023	11,557
Other British Possessions	47,043	52,303	50,044
Total to British Possessions	590,330	584,694	590,019
Total	955,774	1,013,837	1,009,653

Toilet Soap.

	1904.	1905.	1906.
	£	£	£
To Germany	5,051	6,322	6,620
Belgium	3,730	3,265	3,355
France	7,903	8,988	9,324
Portuguese East Africa	2,215	3,973	4,658
Egypt	2,302	3,350	3,525
China (exclusive of Hong-Kong and Macao)	3,096	3,115	3,645
Japan (including Formosa)	3,300	4,649	3,382
United States	50,043	50,668	52,124
Brazil	1,879	2,241	2,292
Other Foreign Countries	22,002	26,081	29,214
Total to Foreign Countries	101,521	112,652	118,139
To Cape of Good Hope	14,094	14,815	14,988
Natal	8,897	11,913	7,280
British India—			
Bombay (including Kurachi)	24,665	24,672	28,316
Madras	4,333	5,851	6,624
Bengal, Eastern Bengal and Assam	14,129	16,021	15,969
Burmah	3,299	3,400	4,667

Straits Settlements and Dependencies	3,590	5,092	4,798
Ceylon and Dependencies	12,210	11,118	12,854
Australia—			
Western Australia	1,549	1,394	1,137
South Australia, (including Northern Territory)	895	644	637
Victoria	11,989	13,614	12,774
New South Wales	3,920	4,278	4,139
Queensland	957	1,097	1,108
Tasmania	482	315	547
New Zealand	5,093	4,498	5,503
Canada	6,382	6,196	8,185
Other British Possessions	11,069	10,855	13,521
Total to British Possessions	127,053	135,773	143,047
Total	228,574	248,425	261,186

The following statistics extracted from official consular reports, etc., show the extent of the soap industry in other parts of the world.

United States.—According to the *Oil, Paint and Drug Report* the total production of soap in the United States during 1905, exclusive of soap products to the value of $1,437,118 made in establishments engaged primarily in the manufacture of other products, reached a value of $68,274,700, made up in the following manner: —

	Quantity.	Value.

	Lbs.	$
Hard soaps	...	56,878,486
Tallow soap	846,753,798	32,610,850
Olein soap	29,363,376	1,363,636
Foots soap	85,000,133	3,090,312
Toilet soaps, including medicated, shaving, and other special soaps	130,225,417	9,607,276
Powdered soaps, sold as such	120,624,968	4,358,682
All other soaps	143,390,957	6,097,670
Soft soap	33,613,416	667,064
Special soap articles	...	554,881

France.—This country exported common soap during 1906 to the value of £556,000, or £8,000 more than in 1905.

The chief centre of the soap industry is Marseilles, which, with about fifty soap factories, produces annually some 3,000,000 cwts.

Germany imported in 1905 soap and perfumery to the value of £3,032, that exported amounting to £15,364.

In Saxony there are eighty soap factories.

Russia.—There are fifty large soap factories in Russia, the annual output from which is about 2,250,000 cwt.

Roumania.—This country possesses about 230 small and eighteen large soap and candle factories, most of which produce only common soap, there being only one firm—in Bucharest—which makes milled soaps.

Denmark.—In this country there are some 200 small soap factories.

Australia.—According to a Board of Trade report, there were ninety-eight soap and candle factories in Australia in 1905, employing 1,568 hands, and producing 495,036 cwt. of soap.

Queensland.—In 1905 this country contained twenty-one soap and candle works, in which 142 hands were employed, and having an output valued at £86,324.

Hong-Kong.—There are about twenty-four soap factories on this island.

Japan.—A Swiss consular report states that in Japan there are now some fifty soap works, producing about 15,000,000 tablets monthly.

Fiji Islands.—These possess only one soap factory, the output from which is 9 cwt. daily.

The following table, compiled from various consular and other official returns, shows the quantity and value of soap imported into different countries and places during the years 1905-7: —

Place and Date.	Household.		Toilet.		Total.	
	Quantity.	Value.	Quantity.	Value.	Quantity.	Value.
Europe—						
Cyprus, 1905	...	...	...	...	...	£9,983
Iceland, 1906	...	...	...	...	...	£6,423
Switzerland, 1906	...	...	...	...	1,702,800 kilos.	...
Turkey	...	...	...	...	About 1,800,000 lb. per annum	...

Africa—						
Algeria, 1906	13,609 tons	£228,640	...	...	...	...
Cape Colony, 1906	15,897,800 lb.	£145,000	427,600 lb.	...	...	...
Gold Coast, 1906	...	...	...	...	...	£23,987
Lourenço, Marques, 1906	357,638 lb.	£4,293	36,000 lb.	£2,195	...	...
Natal, 1906	4,263,000 lb.	...	9,870 lb.	...	...	...
Orange River Colony, 1906	2,382,000 lb.	£23,000	1,748 lb.	...	...	...
Pemba, 1905	...	...	...	...	...	£1,092
Rhodesia, 1906	257,600 lb.	...	2,909 lb.	...	...	...
Southern Nigeria, 1905	...	...	...	...	...	£11,990
Tangier	...	...	...	...	...	£4,554
Transvaal, 1906	4,407,000 lb.	£81,000	202,200 lb.	...	...	...
Tripoli, 1905	...	...	...	...	...	£6,080
Tunis, 1906	...	...	...	...	1,539 tons	£23,727
Zanzibar, 1906	...	...	...	...	...	£6,102
America—						
Bahia, 1906	...	...	...	...	1,031 tons	606,046 milreis
Brazil, 1906	...	...	...	...	1,782 tons from U.K.	...
British Guiana, 1906-7	...	...	...	...	...	£13,733
Canada, 1906-7	...	...	...	...	...	$600,999
Columbia,						

1906—						
Cartagena	...	...	...	...	65,991 tons	...
Barranquilla	...	...	...	...	814,671 lb.	$14,712
Costa Rica, 1906	...	...	...	...	...	£1,269 from U.K.
Ecuador, 1904	...	...	...	...	759,034 kilos.	...
Granada, 1905	...	...	...	...	...	£3,867
Guatemala, 1906	...	£900	...	...	...	...
Martinique, 1906	693,269 kilos.	£6,955	...	...	...	...
Mexico, 1905-6	...	£5,982	...	...	...	...
San Domingo, 1906	...	...	...	...	754,587 lb.	...
St. Vincent, 1905-6	...	...	...	...	...	£1,375
Surinam, 1906	...	£3,905	1,142 tons	...	...	...
Trinidad, 1906-7	...	...	...	...	...	£29,967
United States, 1905	...	$399,797	...	$1,071,446	...	$1,471,243
Asia--						
Ceylon, 1906	...	...	...	...	...	423,700 rupees
China, 1906	...	...	...	...	...	£216,042
Hangchow, 1906	...	...	...	...	...	£5,888
India, 1906-7	...	...	...	...	183,998 cwts.	£215,210
Kiungchow, 1905	...	£575	...	...	...	...

Shanghai, 1905	...	...	...	...	...	£93,256	
Smyrna, 1906	...	...	...	...	261 tons	...	
Australasia--							
Australia, 1906	...	...	891,117 lb.	£65,840	...	...	
Fiji, 1906	...	...	...	...	...	£1,760	
New Zealand, 1905	...	...	...	...	...	£36,843	
Philippine Islands, 1905	...	...	...	...	...	£9,137	

Exports.

	Household.		Toilet.		Total	
Place and Date	Quantity.	Value.	Quantity.	Value.	Quantity.	Value
Europe--						
Candia, Crete, 1906	...	...	...	...	2,200 tons.	£34,000
Greece	...	...	...	...	...	About 500,000 Fr. per annum.
Italy, 1907	3,992,800 kilos.	£95,840	...	...	...	...
Leghorn, 1906	...	...	...	...	1,521 tons.	£37,065
Spain, 1905	4,750,996 kilos.	£98,840	...	...	...	...
Switzerland, 1906	...	...	...	...	77,300 kilos.	...
Africa--						
Cape Colony, 1906	200 lb.	...	...	...	...	...

Natal, 1906	75,225 lb.	...	...	...	...	...
Seychelles, 1906	...	...	...	...	419,329 kilos.	129,590 Rs.
America--						
New Orleans, 1906	...	...	...	...	...	£55,534
Perambuco, 1906	...	...	...	...	3,582 tons.	1,087,797,150 rei.
United States, 1905	44,110,949 lb.	...	...	$1,042,185	...	...
Asia--						
Japan, 1906	...	...	...	...	...	£83,877
Smyrna, 1906	...	...	...	...	322 tons.	...

APPENDIX A.

COMPARISON OF DEGREES, TWADDELL AND BAUMÉ, WITH ACTUAL DENSITIES.

Tw.	B.	Density.	Tw.	B.	Density.	Tw.	B.	Density.	Tw.	B.	Density.
0	0	1.000	44	26.0	1.220	88	44.1	1.440	131	57.1	1.655
1	0.7	1.005	45	26.4	1.225	89	44.4	1.445	132	57.4	1.660
2	1.4	1.010	46	26.9	1.230	90	44.8	1.450	133	57.7	1.665
3	2.1	1.015	47	27.4	1.235	91	45.1	1.455	134	57.9	1.670
4	2.7	1.020	48	27.9	1.240	92	45.4	1.460	135	58.2	1.675
5	3.4	1.025	49	28.4	1.245	93	45.8	1.465	136	58.4	1.680
6	4.1	1.030	50	28.8	1.250	94	46.1	1.470	137	58.7	1.685
7	4.7	1.035	51	29.3	1.255	95	46.4	1.475	138	58.9	1.690
8	5.4	1.040	52	29.7	1.260	96	46.8	1.480	139	59.2	1.695
9	6.0	1.045	53	30.2	1.265	97	47.1	1.485	140	59.5	1.700
10	6.7	1.050	54	30.6	1.270	98	47.4	1.490	141	59.7	1.705
11	7.4	1.055	55	31.1	1.275	99	47.8	1.495	142	60.0	1.710
12	8.0	1.060	56	31.5	1.280	100	48.1	1.500	143	60.2	1.715
13	8.7	1.065	57	32.0	1.285	101	48.4	1.505	144	60.4	1.720
14	9.4	1.070	58	32.4	1.290	102	48.7	1.510	145	60.6	1.725
15	10.0	1.075	59	32.8	1.295	103	49.0	1.515	146	60.9	1.730
16	10.6	1.080	60	33.3	1.300	104	49.4	1.520	147	61.1	1.735
17	11.2	1.085	61	33.7	1.305	105	49.7	1.525	148	61.4	1.740
18	11.9	1.090	62	34.2	1.310	106	50.0	1.530	149	61.6	1.745
19	12.4	1.095	63	34.6	1.315	107	50.3	1.535	150	61.8	1.750
20	13.0	1.100	64	35.0	1.320	108	50.6	1.540	151	62.1	1.755
21	13.6	1.105	65	35.4	1.325	109	50.9	1.545	152	62.3	1.760
22	14.2	1.110	66	35.8	1.330	110	51.2	1.550	153	62.5	1.765
23	14.9	1.115	67	36.2	1.335	111	51.5	1.555	154	62.8	1.770
24	15.4	1.120	68	36.6	1.340	112	51.8	1.560	155	63.0	1.775
25	16.0	1.125	69	37.0	1.345	113	52.1	1.565	156	63.2	1.780

26	16.5	1.130	70	37.4	1.350	114	52.4	1.570	157	63.5	1.785
27	17.1	1.135	71	37.8	1.355	115	52.7	1.575	158	63.7	1.790
28	17.7	1.140	72	38.2	1.360	116	53.0	1.580	159	64.0	1.795
29	18.3	1.145	73	38.6	1.365	117	53.3	1.585	160	64.2	1.800
30	18.8	1.150	74	39.0	1.370	118	53.6	1.590	161	64.4	1.805
31	19.3	1.155	75	39.4	1.375	119	53.9	1.595	162	64.6	1.810
32	19.8	1.160	76	39.8	1.380	120	54.1	1.600	163	64.8	1.815
33	20.3	1.165	77	40.1	1.385	121	54.4	1.605	164	65.0	1.820
34	20.9	1.170	78	40.5	1.390	122	54.7	1.610	165	65.2	1.825
35	21.4	1.175	79	40.8	1.395	123	55.0	1.615	166	65.5	1.830
36	22.0	1.180	80	41.2	1.400	124	55.2	1.620	167	65.7	1.835
37	22.5	1.185	81	41.6	1.405	125	55.5	1.625	168	65.9	1.840
38	23.0	1.190	82	42.0	1.410	126	55.8	1.630	169	66.1	1.845
39	23.5	1.195	83	42.3	1.415	127	56.0	1.635	170	66.3	1.850
40	24.0	1.200	84	42.7	1.420	128	56.3	1.640	171	66.5	1.855
41	24.5	1.205	85	43.1	1.425	129	56.6	1.645	172	66.7	1.860
42	25.0	1.210	86	43.4	1.430	130	56.9	1.650	173	67.0	1.865
43	25.5	1.215	87	48.8	1.435						

(From *The Oil and Colour Trades Journal* Diary.)

APPENDIX B.

COMPARISON OF DIFFERENT THERMOMETRIC SCALES.

Cent.	Fahr.	Cent.	Fahr.	Cent.	Fahr.	Cent.	Fahr.
-40	-40	2	35.6	44	111.2	86	186.8
39	38.2	3	87.4	45	113	87	188.6
38	36.4	4	39.2	46	114.8	88	190.4
37	34.6	5	41	47	116.6	89	192.2
36	32.8	6	42.8	48	118.4	90	194
35	31	7	44.6	49	120.2	91	195.8
34	29.2	8	46.4	50	122	92	197.6
33	27.4	9	48.2	51	123.8	93	199.4
32	25.6	10	50	52	125.6	94	201.2
31	23.8	11	51.8	53	127.4	95	203
30	22	12	58.6	54	129.2	96	204.8
29	20.2	13	55.4	55	131	97	206.6
28	18.4	14	57.2	56	132.8	98	208.4
27	16.6	15	59	57	134.6	99	210.2
26	14.8	16	60.8	58	136.4	100	212
25	13	17	62.6	59	138.2	101	213.8
24	11.2	18	64.4	60	140	102	215.6
23	9.4	19	66.2	61	141.8	+103	+217.4
22	7.6	20	68	62	143.6	104	219.2
21	5.8	21	69.8	63	145.4	105	221
20	4	22	71.6	64	147.2	106	222.8
19	2.2	23	73.4	65	149	107	224.6

18	0.4	24	75.2	66	150.8	108	226.4
17	+1.4	25	77	67	152.6	109	228.2
16	3.2	26	78.8	+68	+154.4	+110	+230
15	5	27	80.6	69	156.2	111	231.8
14	6.8	28	82.4	70	158	112	283.6
13	8.6	29	84.2	71	159.8	113	235.4
12	10.4	30	86	72	161.6	114	237.2
11	12.2	31	87.8	73	163.4	115	239
10	14	+32	+89.6	74	165.2	+116	+240.8
9	15.8	33	91.4	75	167	117	242.6
8	17.6	34	93.2	76	168.8	118	244.4
7	19.4	35	95	77	170.6	119	246.2
6	21.2	36	96.8	78	172.4	120	248
5	23	37	98.6	79	174.2	121	249.8
4	24.8	49	100.4	80	176	+122	+251.6
3	26.6	39	102.2	81	177.8	123	253.4
2	28.4	40	104	82	179.6	124	255.2
1	30.2	41	105.8	83	181.4	125	257
0	32	42	107.6	84	183.2	126	258.8
+1	33.8	43	109.4	85	185	127	260.6

(From *Soaps*, by G. H. Hurst, published by Scott, Greenwood & Son.)

APPENDIX C.

TABLE OF THE SPECIFIC GRAVITIES OF SOLUTIONS OF CAUSTIC SODA.

Degrees Twaddell.	Specific gravity.	Per cent. by weight of		Lb. of actual NaOH contained in 1 gallon of lye made from commercial caustic of		
		Na_2O.	NaOH.	77 per cent.	74 per cent.	70 per cent.
1	1.005	0.368	0.474	0.048	0.046	0.043
2	1.010	0.742	0.957	0.097	0.092	0.087
3	1.015	1.114	1.436	0.146	0.131	0.129
4	1.020	1.480	1.909	0.194	0.185	0.180
5	1.025	1.834	2.365	0.243	0.231	0.219
6	1.030	2.194	2.830	0.291	0.278	0.262
7	1.035	2.521	3.252	0.335	0.320	0.303
8	1.040	2.964	3.746	0.389	0.371	0.350
9	1.045	3.244	4.184	0.438	0.417	0.393
10	1.050	3.590	4.631	0.486	0.461	0.438
11	1.055	3.943	5.086	0.536	0.510	0.483
12	1.060	4.292	5.536	0.586	0.558	0.528
13	1.065	4.638	5.982	0.636	0.607	0.573
14	1.070	4.972	6.413	0.680	0.653	0.617

15	1.075	5.311	6.911	0.742	0.707	0.668
16	1.080	5.648	7.285	0.786	0.749	0.709
17	1.085	5.981	7.715	0.836	0.798	0.755
18	1.090	6.311	8.140	0.886	0.845	0.800
19	1.095	6.639	8.564	0.937	0.894	0.846
20	1.100	6.954	8.970	0.986	0.941	0.890
21	1.105	7.276	9.386	1.037	0.989	0.938
22	1.110	7.594	9.796	1.087	1.037	0.981
23	1.115	7.910	10.203	1.137	1.123	1.026
24	1.120	8.223	10.607	1.187	1.175	1.071
25	1.125	8.583	11.107	1.238	1.181	1.117
26	1.130	8.893	11.471	1.296	1.237	1.170
27	1.135	9.251	11.933	1.354	1.292	1.122
28	1.140	9.614	12.401	1.413	1.350	1.277
29	1.145	9.965	12.844	1.470	1.413	1.337
30	1.150	10.313	13.303	1.529	1.460	1.381
31	1.155	10.666	13.859	1.600	1.528	1.445
32	1.160	11.008	14.190	1.646	1.541	1.456
33	1.165	11.347	14.637	1.705	1.627	1.539
34	1.170	11.691	15.081	1.764	1.684	1.593
35	1.175	12.025	15.512	1.822	1.739	1.645
36	1.180	12.356	16.139	1.904	1.817	1.719
37	1.185	12.692	16.372	1.942	1.853	1.753

Degrees Twaddell.	Specific gravity.	Per cent. by weight of		Lb. of actual NaOH contained in 1 gallon of lye made from commercial caustic of		
		Na_2O.	NaOH.	77 per cent.	74 per cent.	70 per cent.
38	1.190	13.016	16.794	1.998	1.887	1.804
39	1.195	13.339	17.203	2.055	1.962	1.856
40	1.200	13.660	17.629	2.122	2.026	1.916
41	1.205	14.058	18.133	2.185	2.085	1.973
42	1.210	14.438	18.618	2.252	2.147	2.033
43	1.215	14.823	19.121	2.323	2.221	2.097
44	1.220	15.124	19.613	2.392	2.280	2.161
45	1.225	15.502	19.997	2.444	2.338	2.206
46	1.230	15.959	20.586	2.562	2.417	2.285
47	1.235	16.299	20.996	2.593	2.475	2.341
48	1.240	16.692	21.532	2.669	2.548	2.410
49	1.245	17.060	22.008	2.739	2.615	2.474
50	1.250	17.424	22.476	2.809	2.681	2.536
51	1.255	17.800	22.962	2.881	2.750	2.602
52	1.260	18.166	23.433	2.952	2.818	2.666
53	1.265	18.529	23.901	3.020	2.886	2.730

54	1.270	18.897	24.376	3.095	2.955	2.795
55	1.275	19.255	24.858	3.171	3.027	2.863
56	1.280	19.609	25.295	3.237	3.090	2.932
57	1.285	19.961	25.750	3.308	3.158	2.988
58	1.290	20.318	26.210	3.381	3.227	3.053
59	1.295	20.655	26.658	3.452	3.364	3.117
60	1.300	21.156	27.110	3.524	3.394	3.182
61	1.305	21.405	27.611	3.603	3.439	3.253
62	1.310	21.785	28.105	3.682	3.514	3.224
63	1.315	22.168	28.595	3.760	3.593	3.395
64	1.320	22.556	29.161	3.849	3.674	3.475
65	1.325	22.926	29.574	3.919	3.742	3.539
66	1.330	23.310	30.058	3.997	3.816	3.610
67	1.335	23.670	30.535	4.072	3.891	3.681
68	1.340	24.046	31.018	4.156	3.967	3.754
69	1.345	24.410	31.490	4.232	4.042	3.824
70	1.350	24.765	31.948	4.312	4.116	3.894
71	1.355	25.152	32.446	4.396	4.196	3.970
72	1.360	25.526	32.930	4.478	4.274	4.043
73	1.365	25.901	33.415	4.561	4.354	4.109
74	1.370	26.285	33.905	4.645	4.434	4.194
75	1.375	26.650	34.382	4.728	4.513	4.269
76	1.380	27.021	34.855	4.810	4.592	4.344

77	1.385	27.385	35.328	4.893	4.670	4.418
78	1.390	27.745	35.795	4.975	4.794	4.493
79	1.395	28.110	36.258	5.058	4.828	4.567
80	1.400	28.465	36.720	5.141	4.907	4.642
81	1.405	28.836	37.203	5.227	4.989	4.720
82	1.410	29.203	37.674	5.312	5.071	4.797
83	1.415	29.570	38.146	5.397	5.135	4.873
84	1.420	29.930	38.610	5.482	5.233	4.950
85	1.425	30.285	39.071	5.567	5.314	5.027
86	1.430	30.645	39.530	5.653	5.396	5.104
87	1.435	30.995	39.986	5.738	5.467	5.181
88	1.440	31.349	40.435	5.823	5.558	5.258
89	1.445	31.700	40.882	5.908	5.640	5.335
90	1.450	32.043	41.335	5.923	5.721	5.412
91	1.455	32.460	41.875	6.093	5.816	5.502
92	1.460	32.870	42.400	6.191	5.909	5.608
93	1.465	33.283	42.935	6.290	6.004	5.679
94	1.470	33.695	43.467	6.389	6.009	5.769
95	1.475	34.092	43.980	6.487	6.193	5.856
96	1.480	34.500	44.505	6.586	6.287	5.948
97	1.485	34.899	45.013	6.685	6.381	6.035
98	1.490	35.245	45.530	6.784	6.476	6.126
99	1.495	35.691	46.041	6.884	6.571	6.216

| 100 | 1.500 | 36.081 | 46.545 | 6.982 | 6.665 | 6.303 |

(From *Soaps*, by G. H. Hurst, published by Scott, Greenwood & Son.)

APPENDIX D.

TABLE OF STRENGTH OF CAUSTIC POTASH SOLUTIONS AT 60° F.

Specific gravity.	Degrees Twaddell.	Per cent. KOH.	Lb. of KOH per gal.
1.060	12	5.59	0.59
1.110	22	11.31	1.25
1.150	30	15.48	1.77
1.190	38	19.29	2.21
1.230	46	23.22	2.84
1.280	56	27.87	3.56
1.330	66	31.32	4.16
1.360	72	35.01	4.76
1.390	78	38.59	5.36
1.420	84	40.97	5.81
1.440	88	43.83	6.31
1.470	94	47.16	6.93
1.520	104	51.09	7.76
1.600	112	55.62	8.89
1.680	136	60.98	10.24
1.780	156	67.65	12.04
1.880	176	75.74	14.23
2.000	200	86.22	17.24

(From *Soaps*, by G. H. Hurst, published by Scott, Greenwood & Son.)

www.ingramcontent.com/pod-product-compliance
Lightning Source LLC
Chambersburg PA
CBHW071153160426
43196CB00011B/2067